KEY CHANGES TO FAMILY JUSTICE

Shefali Shah

Published by
CoramBAAF Adoption and Fostering Academy
41 Brunswick Square
London WC1N 1AZ
www.corambaaf.org.uk

Coram Academy Limited, registered as a company limited by guarantee in England and Wales
number 9697712, part of the Coram group, charity number 312278

© Shefali Shah, 2016

British Library Cataloguing in Publication Data
A catalogue record for this book is available from the British Library

ISBN 978 1 910039 43 4

Project management by Jo Francis, Publications Department, CoramBAAF
Designed by Helen Joubert Designs
Printed in Great Britain by TJ International

Trade distribution by Turnaround Publisher Services, Unit 3, Olympia Trading Estate, Coburg Road,
London N22 6TZ

Contents

Note about the author

Shefali Shah is a practising solicitor with over 21 years' experience in children law. She has been an accredited member of the Law Society's Children Panel accreditation scheme since 2003. She has over 17 years' experience as a local authority solicitor and manager. She is legal adviser to Adoption UK, Adopters for Adoption and is one of the four legal advisers to the Independent Review Mechanism for England.

She is a member of CoramBAAF's Legal Group Advisory Committee. Shefali is also a national trainer and teaches children law academically on the undergraduate law programme and on the postgraduate legal practice course. She has developed extensive training courses on public children and social care law, and regularly writes legal briefing notes and articles on children law. Further information can be found at www.kingsleyknight.co.uk.

Acknowledgements

I would like to thank all the social care professionals (too numerous to mention by name, but you will know who you are) who have participated in an interactive way in the legal training that I have delivered. By sharing experiences, observations and examples of good practice, raising interesting questions or discussion points, you have helped to contribute to many chapters in this guide.

I would also like to thank everyone at CoramBAAF who helped in the creation of this guide. In particular, I would like to express my gratitude to Alexandra Conroy Harris (Legal Consultant) for finding time to read and comment on the draft. I am also immensely grateful to Shaila Shah (Director of Publications), and Jo Francis (Editor) who, with their professional skill, have transformed this guide into an excellently designed publication.

Finally, I want to thank my dear husband and daughter for their patience and for tolerating my laptop and promises of 'I am nearly done' during weekends and holidays.

Without all of them, this guide would not have been possible.

Introduction

It is often mistakenly said of the family justice system that nothing really changes. However, in 2014 we witnessed some of the biggest, and some would say revolutionary, changes to the system. They are radical reforms with the implementation of far-reaching legislation. These have clearly been interesting times for those involved in family justice and, as the President of the Family Division, Sir James Munby (hereafter referred to as the President) states, this is the start of a "cultural revolution".

The purpose of this guide is to support practitioners, professionals and anyone who is involved in the family justice process by providing an understanding of these recent changes in the law applicable in England and, more importantly, how these changes are being applied in practice. The guide is based on current practice at the time of writing (January 2016). However, it must be noted that practice can vary and may be adapted in different areas or regions. This can depend on local practice, which may have developed based on the lead taken by the Designated Judge, or agreed practice by the local lawyers, CAFCASS (Children and Families Advisory Support Service) and other professionals practising in that particular area.

The Children and Families Act 2014 has had the most far-reaching impact on a number of areas affecting families since the Children Act 1989. The enactment of the Crime and Courts Act 2013 created for the first time the new single Family Court. The Care Act 2014 makes important changes for children who are carers or who may need services from adult social services when they become adults. All of these statutes bring about changes that affect children, which will be explored in greater detail in this guide. These are extremely exciting times for all those involved in the family justice system.

You may ask why all these changes are necessary. In order for the law to remain applicable to modern day society it must be dynamic, because society is ever-changing and so for the law to be relevant it cannot remain static. Society has seen fundamental changes to our understanding of what a nuclear family looks like today. Parents may choose to be married or unmarried, or be in a relationship but choose not to live in the same household. We now have legal recognition of marriage and civil partnership of same-sex couples. Children may have parents who undertake their children's care but may choose to live separately, or the children may have carers who are single parents or parents from same-sex couples. Family law reform therefore needs to reflect these changes to be relevant to today's society.

Another reason for reform is to combat that longstanding issue of attempting to reduce significant delays in court proceedings and to speed up access to justice. Delay has been a feature of family cases and a concern since the implementation of the Children Act 1989. The changes introduced in the Children and Families Act 2014 that attempt to tackle the issue of delay are developed from the originating principles set down in the Children Act 1989. The introduction of the single Family Court is considered to also assist in reducing delay by introducing consistency and flexibility once children proceedings have been issued. The Children and Families Act not only advances the principles set out in the Children Act; it also introduces new concepts that further enhance those original principles, keeping children's best interests as the central focus.

Disclaimer

The contents of this guide are for information on some of the key changes in the family justice system and are not intended to be relied upon as legal advice.

The Family Justice Review

The changes detailed in the introduction to this book have come about as a result of many reviews and consultations.

The Family Justice Review, chaired by David Norgrove, was seen as the first step towards the radical changes for the creation of a more streamlined and structured process to achieve long-term improvements for children. The Family Justice Review recommended that the priorities for change should be to speed up process, support parents to resolve disputes and to be child-focused (Family Justice Review Panel, 2011).

As the changes are seen as developing the principles already set down in the Children Act 1989, the changes proposed by the Family Justice Review did not propose amendments to the fundamental principles as set down in the Children Act, and welfare of the child remains paramount.

The Family Justice Review's findings and recommendations were accepted first by the then Government and then by Parliament with the passing of the Children and Families Act 2014. They were then implemented under the collaborative leadership of the judiciary and the Family Justice Board, also chaired by David Norgrove. The Children and Families Act 2014 also had input from the following:

- *An Action Plan for Adoption: Tackling delay* (Department for Education (DfE), March 2012a)

- *Further Action on Adoption: Finding more loving homes* (DfE, January 2013a)

- *The Government Response to the Family Justice Review* (Ministry of Justice (MoJ) and DfE, February 2012)

- *Support and Aspiration: A new approach to special educational needs and disability: Progress and next steps* (DfE, May 2012b)

- *More Great Childcare: Raising quality and giving parents more choice* (DfE, January 2013b)

- *The Government Response to the Modern Workplaces Consultation* (DfE, November 2012c).

The Family Court

Some may take the view that when reform does take place in the legal arena, it can be slow. With regards to the creation of the single Family Court, this could be said to be true. The single Family Court was first proposed over 40 years ago and came into existence on 22 April 2014 with the implementation of the Crime and Courts Act 2013. This means that we no longer have the three-tier court system, as illustrated below:

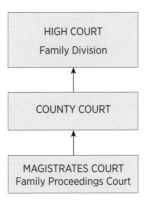

From 22 April 2014, family cases are no longer heard in the Family Proceedings Court or the County Court but are all heard in the newly established single Family Court. This encompasses the Family Proceedings Court, the County Court and the Family Division of the High Court. This means that all the different tiers of family judges (that is, High Court Judges, Circuit Judges, District Judges and Lay Magistrates) now all hear family cases and sit in the Family Court.

Even though we no longer have the Family Proceedings Court, Lay Magistrates still play a key role in the family justice system and, for the first time, under this new regime will sit alongside their judicial colleagues in the Family Court.

Family Court			
Four levels/tiers of Family Court Judges			
High Court Judges	Circuit Judges	District Judges	Lay Magistrates

The Family Court has the jurisdiction to deal with all family cases, with the exception of two classes of cases which are reserved for the Family Divison of the High Court:

a) Wardship and other cases that require the exercise of the inherent jurisdiction of the High Court; and

b) cases of international abduction.

Wherever possible, all the judges of the Family Court will endeavour to sit in the same building; however, if this is not possible, then wherever they sit as a family judge, in whichever building, it will still be known as the Family Court.

For the court, England and Wales continue to be divided into geographical areas; all the locations within each geographical area are judicially led and managed by a senior judge known as the Designated Family Judge. Each Designated Family Centre will have at least one Designated Family Judge who is responsible for the administrative running of the Family Court in their area.

The Family Court in each region will be supported by an administrative court office that will in effect act as a single point of entry for the issue of all family proceedings; this has resulted in a centralised and unified administration.

The result of these changes is that once a case is issued in the Family Court, it will be managed thereafter by the court services in a consistent way by a centralised gate-keeping and allocation team. This Family Court administrative team is responsible for allocating the case before an appropriate tier of judge at an appropriate place.

Why was the single Family Court created?

- The single Family Court is intended to create a much simpler system.

- The new court framework will be easier for individuals acting on their own behalf, so when issuing an application, the applicant will simply submit their application to the Family Court in their area. The applicant will no longer have to ascertain whether they should apply to the Family Proceedings Court, the County Court or the High Court. Once the Family Court has issued the application, it will then allocate the case to a tier of the judiciary, and a judge or magistrates will be allocated to hear the case. If any of the parties object to the area or to the tier, then a request can be made to the court prior to allocation or after allocation.

- The new system is intended to reduce delay and create a modern, efficient, just and speedy family justice system. It means that delays will be reduced with listing of cases and, if necessary, cases can be transferred up or down depending on the tier of judge that is required to hear the case with ease and minimum delay. This ensures that the new structure allows a more effective and efficient use of judges' and courts' time.

Adversarial versus inquisitorial process

Courts in England operate on an adversarial process, and this is still true of the Family Court. However, as part of the delivery of a speedier and more streamlined process, family judges will now no longer operate purely on the old adversarial system of simply leaving it to the parties to steer the direction of the case, but will now take a more inquisitorial approach. Modern case management will now require the family judge to take on the responsibility of deciding on issues such as what will be argued upon, for how long and what evidence will be permitted. This process may still be adversarial; however, it will be clearly managed by the judge and there is a duty for parties to assist in this process. If parties are not legally represented, then the judge may need to take a more active role.

Such a fresh approach is considered to be necessary in order to assist with the age-old issue of reducing delay and ensuring the progress of cases once they are within the court's domain.

Transparency of the Family Courts

Another vital transformation in the family justice system has been in relation to access to and reporting of family cases. These reforms are considered to be necessary to enable the Family Courts to gain public respect and to rid themselves of the damaging public image that the Family Courts operate in private, passing justice in a "secret" way. The President has made it clear that, as part of the radical reforms he has introduced, he also seeks to promote openness and transparency in the Family Courts.

Transparency should not be confused with media access and publicity. As part of the process of increasing the transparency of the family justice system, and to improve public confidence in its operation, from April 2009[1] accredited members of the press have been permitted to attend family hearings, including children cases (with a few exceptions, see later), unless there are good reasons as to why they should not, which the judge will decide upon. The opening of Family Courts for reporters was seen as a historic change. Jack Straw, the then Justice Secretary, stated that this was 'to ensure a change in the culture and practice of all courts towards greater openness'. It was considered to be a step towards ensuring that the Family Court as a public body was being held to account, and was subject to public scrutiny.

Therefore, Family Courts do permit journalists to attend children cases, but this should not be confused with the fact that children cases remain closed cases, and they are not open to the general public, who are not permitted to attend the court hearing.

---

1   *The Family Proceedings (Amendment)(No 2) Rules 2009* SI 2009 No 857 (County Court and High Court) and *The Family Proceedings Courts (Miscellaneous Amendments) Rules 2009* SI 2009 No 858 (Magistrates' Courts)

Members of the press are excluded from certain types of family hearings, such as those concerning applications for parental orders (court orders transferring legal rights from the birth mother to the applicant/s after a surrogacy arrangement) and hearings concerning adoption. Also, the judge has the ability to prevent the press from attending certain hearings or from parts of the hearing, if it is necessary:

- to protect the interests of a child involved in the proceedings; or

- for the safety or protection of a party, witness or persons connected with them; or

- for the "orderly conduct" of the proceedings; or

- where justice would otherwise be impeded or prejudiced.

A judge might therefore decide to remove the media from the courtroom if, for example, he or she considers that a witness may refuse to give evidence with the media present, or if the whereabouts of a vulnerable person might be revealed.

Although attendance of journalists has been permitted in Family Courts since April 2009, there are clear restrictions on what journalists can report on. Journalists are not allowed to name or identify adults or children involved in specific cases, or to report on the details of the case unless they apply for and receive specific permission from the judge. Generally, journalists are limited to reporting the court process and the principles by which decisions are made. The courts have wide powers to protect the interests of children and if journalists do not comply with these strict limits, they can be found to be in contempt of court if they publish information about proceedings without permission. Journalists therefore need to be very careful to ensure that they do not breach the rules.

Transparency of the courts must be considered in the context of Articles 6 and 8 of the European Convention of Human Rights (ECHR), balanced with Article 10, the right to freedom of expression. So although the rules permit journalists to be in court and allow them to report on the court's workings and reasoning (which is what the public may want from the press), the

Article 10 right to freedom of expression must be balanced with the rules that restrict the journalists so that the individuals or family's rights under Article 8 (respecting private lives and identities of private parties) are not breached without the court's permission. These competing rights will also be considered in light of Article 6 (parties' right to a fair hearing).

In general, although the rules permitting the admittance of journalists did initially concern professionals, in practice very few cases attract media interest unless they are of a high profile nature. One reason for this is that the current rules do not give journalists the right to see any documents produced for the court and so it may be difficult for journalists to follow or understand what may be going on in the case or at that hearing, without access to the court documentation.

If any party, professional or even a witness is concerned about the presence of journalists or media coverage in a family case, then they should seek legal advice from either their legal representative (if they are a party) or the legal representative who has requested them to attend court (if they are a witness or an expert witness). This should be done preferably before the hearing so that the judge can consider directions in relation to the reporters, or only grant restricted access by the press for part or all of the hearing.

The changes in April 2009 were seen by some as a radical step towards transparency; however, we have moved on since then. Further steps in relation to greater transparency were announced initially in April 2013, with the President issuing a statement[2] in which he said:

> I am determined to take steps to improve access to and reporting of family proceedings. I am determined that the new Family Court should not be saddled, as the family courts are at present, with the charge that we are a system of secret and unaccountable justice.

In January 2014, the President issued Practice Guidance on the publication of judgements to his senior judges regarding judgements made in the Family Courts and in the Court of Protection, which came into effect on 3 February

---

2   'View from the President's Chambers: the Process of Reform' [2013] *Fam Law* 548

2014 (Munby, 2014a). This guidance advised senior judges to make more of their judgements available to the public, unless there were compelling reasons as to why the judgement should not be published. The intention for this change was to improve public understanding of the court process and increase confidence in the court system, supporting the view that greater publication of judgements will make for greater transparency.

When the judge is deciding whether or not to publish a judgement at the conclusion of the case, he or she will have regard to all the circumstances, including rights arising from the relevant provisions under the ECHR such as Article 6 (right to a fair hearing), Article 8 (respect for private and family life) and Article 10 (freedom of expression), and the effect of publication on any current or potential criminal proceedings.

A recent example of where reporting restrictions were lifted was in *Roger Williams v Rebecca Minnock and Ethan Freeman Williams*, which concerned the question of with whom a child was to live. In this case, not only were all the eight judgements[3] made available to the public, but also the judge made the unusual step of permitting the press to print the names of the parents and the child and details of the case in order to secure the child's whereabouts. In this case, the mother went on the run with her three-year-old son after the court ruled in private law children proceedings that the child was to live with his father. The hunt for the child ended after 17 days when the mother handed herself in after speaking to the press. The judge responded to the mother's comments by stating that:

I think it is important the public understands the seriousness with which the court approaches the task of ensuring if at all possible that both parents maintain an effective relationship with the child.[4]

It should be noted that in light of the guidance issued in January 2014, public authorities and expert witnesses can be personally named unless there are compelling reasons why they should not be. Publication of the

3   *Roger Williams v Rebecca Minnock and Ethan Freeman Williams* (eight judgements), 15 June 2015 Case No: VS13P00027 Bristol Crown Court
4   Reported in *The Guardian*, 12 June 2015

names of local authorities and expert witnesses, which can include not just independent expert witnesses but also social workers, could have an impact on professionals when working with other families, and possible wider implications. If professionals are concerned about the impact the publication of their names may have, they should consult their legal representative if they are a party, or the legal representative who has requested them to provide a report or to attend court, to consider whether directions in relation to restricting publication can be made prior to the conclusion of the proceedings or the hearing.

Further to the President's guidance and as part of his agenda to promote greater openness and transparency in the Family Courts, the President set out his aims and views as to how to extend the existing guidance. This was issued in January 2014 in a consultation paper, *Transparency: The next steps*, which was published in September 2014 (Munby, 2014b).[5] The consultation paper focused on:

(1) (i) *the impact on children and families, both immediate, short term and long term;*

(ii) *the impact on local authorities and other professionals; and*

(iii) *any change in the level and quality of news and reporting about the family justice system.*

(2) *Views and suggestions regarding information on listing of cases.*

(3) *Proposed further guidance on the disclosure of documents, subject to appropriate restrictions and safeguards, to enable the media to better understand the case and assist them in performing their "watchdog" role.*

(4) *Preliminary, pre-consultation views about the possible hearing in public of certain types of family case.*

Those supporting greater transparency take the view that the public demands information, particularly with high profile cases. Journalists facing that public pressure would be forced to print whatever information they can. The

5   [2014] *Fam Law* 1331

concern is that, if that information is not correct or fully correct, once printed or broadcasted it would be out in the public domain. Thereafter, if and once the correct information is available, it may be difficult to retract the incorrect information. Further, although there is some ability to control the printed press or what is broadcast, there is very limited opportunity to control what may be available on the internet, and for that reason it is important to be able to make the correct information available from the outset.

The President made it clear that he is anxious with regard to all aspects of transparency, and requested to hear from all who have been through, or know of others who have been through, the family justice system, including the views and experiences of children and young people. There has been strong opposition to greater transparency from many organisations, including the Children's Commissioner for England and the National Youth Advocacy Service (NYAS). Those opposing this increased transparency agenda do so on the basis of the need to protect the privacy of children/young people who are subject to proceedings. They take the view that general rules about publicity would not be helpful and that cases should be considered individually.

At the time of writing, the President's response to the consultation paper is still awaited. In light of the strong opposition, matters will have to be considered very carefully regarding how further transparency can be achieved. Consideration will also have to be given not only to the short-term but also to the long-term consequences that further disclosure may have on families, particularly on the issue of children's privacy. Disclosure permitted at the time may be considered to be the right decision for the child; however, consideration will also have to be given to the possible long-term impact of disclosure on the child's privacy and life as they grow older or even when they are an adult.

Legal aid

Public proceedings

For parties who are involved in pre-proceedings or during care or supervision order proceedings, legal aid is automatically available to those who have parental responsibility.

The entitlement of legal aid is not means- or merit-tested.

Pre-proceedings

Once a local authority has decided to commence the PLO process, it should notify the parents or carers by serving a notice before court proceedings letter (see Chapter 5 for more information). Any parent or carer who has parental responsibility and who is served with this formal notice letter will then be automatically entitled to Level 2 legal help. This will entitle the parent or carer to legal advice and the support of a solicitor at no cost. This will even entitle the parent or carer to receive support from a solicitor during the pre-proceedings stage of the Public Law Outline (PLO), including attendance at the PLO meeting with the local authority.

Post-commencement of proceedings

If the local authority then progresses to commencing care or supervision order proceedings, the parent, carer or any party with parental responsibility will be entitled to fully funded legal representation.

Private proceedings

There have been major changes to the eligibility and availability of legal aid for private law children proceedings, which took effect in April of 2013. These changes have resulted in legal aid no longer being available in private law proceedings unless there is evidence of domestic violence. Due to this limited availability, professionals (particularly social workers, GPs or the police) may be requested to provide evidence of referrals of domestic violence, which will assist in providing the required evidence to those who are alleging domestic violence in their application for legal aid.

McKenzie Friends

The restricted availability of legal aid has resulted in an ever-increasing number of litigants in person; that is, individuals bringing or defending applications in the Family Court without legal representation. If a person is not entitled to legal aid, then funding of legal support can be extremely costly for the individual. The non-availability of legal representation by a solicitor due to lack of eligibility of legal aid has resulted in the increase of McKenzie Friends. They are lay persons; that is, they are not legally qualified, but assist the litigant in person, i.e. a person who is a party to the proceedings and who is representing themselves as they do not have legal representation.

McKenzie Friends have no right to:

- act as advocates;
- carry out the conduct of litigation;
- act as the litigant in person's agent in relation to the proceedings;
- manage the litigant in person's case outside court, for example, by signing court documents; or
- address the court, make oral submissions or examine witnesses.

McKenzie Friends can:

- provide moral support to the litigant in person;

- take notes at court;

- help the litigant in person with case papers; and

- quietly give advice on any aspect of the conduct of the case.

Traditionally, McKenzie Friend support has been provided on a voluntary basis by a family member or friend. However, due to the decrease in the availability of legal aid, there has been a steady increase in the use of fee-charging McKenzie Friends, aiming to meet the needs of litigants in person who are not eligible for legal aid funding and who cannot afford legal representation.

The fee-charging McKenzie Friends can be seen as more attractive to the litigant in person as, if they do charge, their fees will be considerably less than employing the services of a solicitor. However, one must remember that a McKenzie Friend is not legally qualified, and although they can assist, there are also restrictions placed on them, as set out above. It should also be remembered that a McKenzie Friend should not be considered to be an alternative to seeking legal representation, as they do not need to have any form of legal qualification and are unregulated. For that reason, anyone can set themselves up as a McKenzie Friend. They are not accountable to any regulated body. They could take on a case and may not take steps in the best interests of the person whom they appear to represent, which could be detrimental to the litigant in person's case. Therefore, very careful consideration should be taken before a litigant in person considers appointing a McKenzie Friend.

The position of a McKenzie Friend is unlike that of a solicitor, who has to serve their client and act in their client's best interests; if a solicitor does not do this, they are accountable to the Solicitor Regulation Authority.

The increase of litigants in person has also placed a burden on the judiciary, who not only have to dispense justice but also have to manage the case due to the absence of legal representatives. The use of a McKenzie Friend can assist the judge in the management of the case. However, if a McKenzie Friend does not remain within the constraints within the judicial guidance,[1] then they could be seen as a hindrance to the court and, as already mentioned, this can be severely detrimental to the litigant in person's case.

1   Judicial guidance for the civil and family courts, issued on 12 July 2010, was authored by Lord Neuberger of Abbotsbury, Master of the Rolls, and Sir Nicholas Wall, President of the Family Division.

5

The Children and Families Act 2014

The biggest changes to the family justice system are as a result of the Children and Families Act 2014. This is a landmark piece of legislation. It received Royal Assent on 13 March 2014, and many of the key provisions came into force, alongside the introduction of the single Family Court, on 22 April 2014.

The changes in this legislation are far-reaching, affecting different aspects of children and family life. The Act changes the law relating to adoption, children looked after by local authorities and the family justice system and impacts on some of the following areas:

- private children law, introduction of the concept of parental involvement and mediations, information and assessment meetings;

- statutory time limits for public law care and supervision order proceedings;

- Fostering to Adopt (also known as early permanence placement);

- special educational needs and the statutory requirement for a virtual school head;

- expansion of the functions of the Children's Commissioner;

- "Staying Put" for children in foster care (when they reach the age of 18);

- shared parental leave and equal employment leave rights for adoptive parents and parents of children born of surrogacy;

- adoption support services;

- recruitment, assessment and approval functions by the local authority;

- the Adoption Register.

The Act reforms the system for looked after children, as well as in relation to adoption and special educational needs. The Act itself consists of 10 parts that cover the following:

Part 1   Adoption and contact
Part 2   Family justice
Part 3   Children and young people with special educational needs or disabilities
Part 4   Child care
Part 5   The welfare of children
Part 6   The Children's Commissioner
Part 7   Statutory rights to employment leave and pay
Part 8   Time off work, antenatal care
Part 9   Right to request flexible working
Part 10   General provisions

For the purposes of this guide, we consider some of the key changes.

Private law Children Act proceedings

Presumption of parental involvement

The Children and Families Act has created a presumption of parental involvement with the introduction of s.11. This sets out a presumption that any parent should be involved in the life of their child in a direct, indirect or supervised manner unless such involvement would not further the child's welfare. This is based on the view that most children benefit from a continuing relationship with both parents, and that shared parenting should be encouraged in cases where this is in the child's best interests, and safe to do so. It also sends out an important message to parents that they play a valuable role in their child's life.

However, it should be noted that this section does not create a presumption of shared parenting or of equal division of time between the parents. The presumption of parental involvement does not assume that parents are entitled to equality when considering issues of contact or residence. The presumption of parental involvement means that both parents should share responsibility for caring for their child, keeping the child's welfare as the paramount consideration. The courts will therefore take into account as a starting position the principle that both separated parents should continue to be involved in their child's life, as long as it is safe to do so. However, it does not assume that the parents have equality and each case will be determined by the facts of the case. Section 11 may require parents and their legal representatives to consider creative solutions when resolving care arrangements, particularly if parents live a long distance away or are not readily available.

It should be noted that, in practical terms, this amendment does not impact on the principles of parental responsibility and only affects the welfare principle enshrined in s.1 of the Children Act 1989, in that s.11(1) of the Children and Families Act 2014 amends s.1 of the Children Act 1989 in relation to the welfare of the child, so that there is a new s.1(2)(A) in the Children Act 1989. This new section has the effect that, in certain situations, unless the contrary is shown, the court is to presume that the involvement of that parent in the life of the child concerned will further the child's welfare.

So when the court is dealing with an application relating to the child, the court will need to consider firstly whether a parent can be involved in the child's life in a way that does not put the child at risk of suffering harm, which may occur as a result of direct or indirect contact. Thereafter, the court will need to consider whether contact should take place, starting from the point that contact with a parent is beneficial to the child unless it can be shown that this presumption should be rebutted because the contact may not further the child's welfare.

It should be noted that the presumption does not apply to certain cases, such as those where the court is considering whether to make public law orders; that is, where there is an application for a care or supervision order, or for a special guardianship order. It also does not apply to applications for an order for the disclosure of a child's whereabouts or an order for the recovery of a child, applied for under ss.33 and 34 respectively in the Family Law Act 1986.

Child arrangements orders

The Family Justice Review recommended that both residence and contact orders should be replaced by a new type of order, known as a child arrangements order. This order sets out the arrangements for the upbringing of a child when the court is faced with making a determination relating to disputes about the care of a child. This recommendation was accepted and has resulted in the creation of a new type of private law order. Section 12 of the Children and Families Act 2014 introduces child arrangements orders, under s.8 of the Children Act 1989. These orders prescribe 'with whom a child is to live, spend time or otherwise have contact' and can be granted to more than one person, whether they live together or not. Child arrangements orders are not limited solely to parents but can also be granted in respect of arrangements between siblings, and extended family members. If a child arrangements order states that the child will live with a person, that person will have parental responsibility for that child until the order ceases. Contact with a child can either be direct, such as face-to-face meetings, or indirect, by way of letters or an exchange of cards, or even by way of online communication. The order can also give directions, for example, if contact is to be supervised by a third person, or if that contact is to take place in a specific location.

Child arrangements orders have therefore replaced contact and residence orders as previously granted under s.8 of the Children Act 1989 and after 22 April 2014, any pre-existing contact or residence orders are deemed to be child arrangements orders. These new orders concentrate more on meeting the "needs" of the child, and less on "parental rights" over the child, and encourage parents to make their own arrangements and only to revert to the court where mediation fails or is not appropriate to use, such as in cases where domestic violence is alleged.

It should be noted that child arrangement orders are still made under s.8 of the Children Act 1989, and that the other s.8 private law orders, namely prohibited steps orders and specific issue orders, remain.

Mediation

There is a sea of cultural change relating to children proceedings and this is equally true in private children law proceedings. The priority is to encourage those parents who are separating and who are in dispute over their child's arrangements to first focus outside the court system to start their journey to resolving their dispute, initially via mediation. It has to be acknowledged that this may not be an easy process for individuals in the midst of separation, particularly when combined with being at their most vulnerable, agonised and even possibly angry with the other parent or party. The use of mediation, and confidence in its success, does therefore require a cultural change. There is now a clear requirement that, unless one of the exemptions applies (see below), then individuals who cannot agree on their child's arrangements need to use mediation (where appropriate to do so) in the first instance, and only if mediation does not assist can individuals then request the court to resolve the issues on which they cannot agree.

As a way to ensure that mediation is considered before the commencement of any private Children Act proceedings, the Children and Families Act prescribes at s.10 that, prior to commencement of any family application, parties must attend a Mediation Information and Assessment Meeting (MIAM) before any relevant family application is made to court. This mandatory requirement will not be applicable if one of the exemptions applies, which includes domestic violence, child protection concerns and urgency. MIAMs provide information and invite prospective litigants to consider mediation and other methods of alternative dispute resolution. The provision applies irrespective of whether the parties are privately funded or in receipt of legal aid. Legal aid can be available for MIAMs to one or both of the parties and each person will be assessed separately. Therefore, individuals considering MIAMs should discuss the issue of eligibility for legal aid and, if they are not eligible, the cost of the mediation with the mediator prior to the first meeting, and the cost of any proceedings that may be commenced if the MIAM is not successful in resolving the dispute.

For those individuals who are relying on one of the exemptions, attendance at a MIAM may not be necessary and those individuals can commence proceedings immediately, if they can satisfy that one of the exemptions applies. Legal aid funding for legal representation may be available if the individual is relying on the exemption; to do so, the individual needs to provide the required evidence.

Public law proceedings

These are proceedings commenced by the local authority and include applications for care and supervision orders. Care proceedings are governed by a case management system known as the Public Law Outline.

Revised Public Law Outline

Do not be mistaken in thinking that the Public Law Outline (PLO) was introduced by the Children and Families Act 2014. The PLO has been around initially in its pilot form since November 2007 and then implemented nationally in April 2008. What the Children and Families Act did was to place the revised PLO on a statutory footing, introducing for the first time a statutory maximum of 26 weeks for the conclusion of care proceedings (subject to a narrowly defined exception).

The revised PLO is a procedural case management system for care cases; it allows the family judges to manage the care proceedings and to dispose of the case without delay. It is not the first case management system that was introduced. Prior to the PLO and the revised PLO, there was the implementation of the Protocol for Judicial Case Management in Public Law Children Act Cases (known as the Judicial Protocol) which was issued in June 2003.[1] The somewhat limited success of the Judicial Protocol resulted in the creation of the PLO and the revised PLO. Both the PLO and the revised PLO initially operated for a pilot period, which assisted in informing the implementation of the final respective versions.

1   2 FLR 719

You may ask, what is the purpose of all these case management systems? In essence, they were introduced as an attempt to reduce unnecessary delay in care proceedings. As has already been mentioned, the question of delay has been present since the implementation of the Children Act 1989. This was noted in the Lord Chancellor's Department's *Scoping Study on Delay in Children Act Cases* (2002), which pointed out:

> When the Children Act 1989 was implemented in 1991, it was anticipated that it would take an average of 12 weeks for care cases to be resolved. This has proved to be over optimistic and has rarely been realised in practice...

The Children Act 1989 has several provisions designed to minimise delay.

- Section 1(2) of the Act requires the court 'to have regard to the general principle that any delay in determining the question is likely to be prejudicial to the child's welfare'.

- Section 32 requires a court hearing in care proceedings 'to draw up a timetable with a view to disposing the application without delay'.

- Section 38 lays down time limits on the making of interim care orders or interim supervision orders.

The revised PLO aims to reduce delay by streamlining the public law process so that all care cases are concluded in 26 weeks unless there are exceptional circumstances. So, once proceedings are issued, it is the court that undertakes the case management responsibility by drawing up a timetable but, equally, while having regard to the impact that the timetable will have on the welfare of the child and the conduct of the proceedings.

The keys to the success of the revised PLO, and its predecessor, the PLO, are:

- firstly, if local authority intervention brings about positive change within the pre-proceedings stage, and a successful outcome is achieved, then court intervention will not be necessary. For such a course of action to be successful, it does require the co-operation of the parents or family members to support the local authority's plan and engage in the services being provided by the local authority during the pre-proceedings stage.

- secondly, if court intervention is necessary then the PLO assists with the management of the case to its final conclusion within the 26 weeks. To achieve the 26 week timescale with the best outcome for the child, this requires all the professionals, parties and their legal representatives to work within the prescribed timescales.

Extension of the 26 week timetable

The real challenge of the PLO is to ensure that the necessary evidence is available to be tested within the 26 week timetable.

It should be noted that the 26 week timetable only starts once the proceedings have been issued and is not applicable for the pre-proceedings stage, which has no statutory timeframe. Also, if the care proceedings are being heard in the Family Drug and Alcohol Court (FDAC), then the 26 week timetable does not apply.

Extensions to the 26 week timetable can be granted,[2] but only if the court considers that the extension is necessary to enable the court to resolve the proceedings justly. Extensions will not be granted routinely, and only on an exceptional basis. The court can extend the period on its own initiative or on application by a party. When a party is requesting an extension, the party will have to justify the reason for which the extension is required and it must be considered at a hearing. There is no limit to the number of extensions that can be granted; however, each will only be granted to a maximum duration of eight weeks.[3]

The President gave examples in the case of *Re S (A Child)* [2014][4] where extensions may be required:

- where it can be identified very early on that a case involves very complex medical evidence and where a separate fact-finding hearing is directed;

2   Section 32(5) Children and Families Act 2014
3   Section 32(8) Children and Families Act 2014
4   *Re S (A Child)* [2014] EWCC B44 (FAM)

- FDAC-type cases where the court is adopting a problem-solving approach;

- cases with an international element, where assessments or investigations abroad are required (this is an important acknowledgement of the recent increase in public law cases involving an international element and recognition of the complications that can arise that may impact on the 26 week timetable);

- where a parent's disabilities require special assessments or measures;

- where, despite robust and vigorous judicial case management, something unexpectedly emerges to change the nature of the proceedings, for example, the case is about neglect or emotional harm but allegations of sexual abuse later surface, or the case is derailed because of a death, serious illness or imprisonment of a proposed carer, or a realistic alternative carer emerges late in the day;

- where litigation failures by one or more of the parties render it impossible to complete the case within 26 weeks.

In order for the 26 week timescale to be met, the court will apply robust case management to the timetable of the care case from the outset. However, the court will also be mindful of the need to balance the time limit with the need to ensure justice for all parties, including the child.

In *Re S (Parenting Assessment)* [2014],[5] the President reiterated that the deadline of 26 weeks can and must be met. The President has also considered Pauffley J's judgement in *Re NL (Interim Care Order: Facts and Reasons)*[6] that 'justice must never be sacrificed upon the altar of speed'. Any extension to the timetable should be determined on a case-by-case basis, and when considering extension of time relating to the parent, typically these questions should be addressed:

- whether there is some solid reason based on evidence to believe that the parent is committed to making the necessary changes within the child's timescale;

5   [2014] EWCC B44 (Fam)
6   [2014] EWHC 270 (Fam), [2014] 2 FLR and reported in April [2014] *Fam Law* 427)

- whether there is some solid reason based on evidence to believe that the parent will be able to maintain that commitment.

Children's lives, like anyone else's, can take unforeseen twists and turns, and perhaps even more so for those subject to care proceedings. Therefore, despite robust and vigorous judicial case management, an unexpected event could change the nature of the proceedings, as detailed in the President's examples provided in *Re S (A Child)* [2014] (detailed above). In such circumstances, extension of the 26 week timetable will have to be given serious consideration by the court, as the particular events in the case have resulted in it being unable to be concluded to a satisfactory resolution within the timeframe. Therefore, in order for the 26 week timetable to be met, the court will need to apply a robust case management to the timetable of the care case from the outset. However, the court will equally need to be mindful of the need to balance the time limit with the need to ensure justice for all parties, including the child. If any party wishes to seek an extension, the party will have to make a formal application to the court setting out the reasons and the period of extension sought.

The PLO places the responsibility of ensuring that the case is concluded within the 26 week timetable on the court and the parties; in order to achieve it, all parties are required to co-operate fully with the court's timetable. If any party fails to co-operate without justification, they could face financial penalties, with the court considering the making of a costs order.

Pre-proceedings and the PLO stages

To assist with the understanding of the PLO, see Appendix 1, which sets out the various stages before the decision is made to commence the PLO process leading to the commencement of proceedings. Appendix 2 shows a flowchart of the various pre-proceedings and PLO stages together with timescales. The days identified in this flowchart are business days and not calendar days. The 26 week time limit means 26 calendar weeks beginning on the day of issue, which is the commencement of proceedings; this being Day 1.

However, it must be remembered that the flowchart in Appendix 2 demonstrates a guide and that each individual case takes its own journey depending on the individual facts of the case and what action is required. To ensure that the PLO process evolves in an organic way depending on the needs of the case, the court has flexible case management powers and can give directions even without having a hearing, and can also list further hearings if needed. This ensures that the court can deal with cases justly in accordance with parties' ECHR Article 6 rights to a fair trial.

Pre-proceedings stage

The PLO process commences with the pre-proceedings stage. It should be remembered that the PLO pre-proceedings requirement does not act as any bar in commencing legal proceedings if the child's welfare requires this. If proceedings have to be commenced immediately, then the pre-proceedings work, such as convening a family group conference or assessments that would have taken place either prior to or during the pre-proceedings stage, will have to be undertaken in the life of the court proceedings.

It is important to note that the PLO does not prevent the safeguarding of children, which must always be the priority. Therefore, the pre-proceedings stage will only be undertaken if the child can be safeguarded during it. If the child is at risk of harm, then the local authority must consider all available options to safeguard the child, which may include commencing legal proceedings immediately. For that reason, there must be a constant monitoring of the balance between safeguarding the child versus work being undertaken in the pre-proceedings stage, and planning towards the possible need for commencement of proceedings. The child's welfare will always take priority over any pre-proceedings timetable.

If steps need to be taken to safeguard the child during the pre-proceedings stage, then prior to consideration of commencement of any proceedings, the local authority children's social care department should consider all other options, which can include placement of the child with family or friends or requesting agreement from those who have parental responsibility to place the child in foster care (under s.20 of the Children Act). This will enable the pre-proceedings stage to be undertaken whilst the child is safeguarded and without the need to commence care proceedings immediately.

It is important to remember that if proceedings do need to be commenced by the local authority immediately in order to safeguard the child's welfare, then that safety should never be compromised due to the fact that court documentation may not be prepared to send to court. The proceedings should be issued by the local authority without delay and the court should be informed as to when any missing annex documents will be filed. The court will then issue directions for the filing of the absent documentation.

As has already been stated, the 26 week timetable does not apply to the pre-proceedings stage. However, it is important that the progress of the pre-proceedings stage is not delayed, and that any delay can be reasonably justified as necessary.

As there is no statutory time limit for the pre-proceedings work, there are concerns that cases may be delayed at this stage. This is one of the areas of concern identified by research commissioned by the Ministry of Justice (2014); that even in pressing cases, some local authorities were not submitting applications until they had all the documentation required. This resulted in the pre-proceedings stage taking longer than it should, leading to potential delay being transferred away from court proceedings to the pre-proceedings stage, with the child left in "legal limbo", with no independent representation to hear the child's voice in this process.

If the local authority causes delay without due justification at the pre-proceedings stage, then the risk is that parents could withdraw their co-operation and, if relevant, their consent for their child to be voluntarily accommodated.[7] By withdrawing their consent, this will require the local authority to either return the child to the parent's care or, if this is not in the child's best interests, and if returning the child to the parent's care could place the child at risk of significant harm, then the local authority will have no alternative but to commence emergency proceedings to safeguard the child.

---

7   Section 20, Children Act 1989

Delay in the pre-proceedings stage could result in breach of the family's Article 8 ECHR rights to a private and family life. It can also result in very limited access to legal advice for the parents, and to the child having no independent representation.

In order to avoid drift and delay at the pre-proceedings stage, some local authorities have developed systems and checks as part of monitoring and good practice. Some have set corresponding 26 week timescales to complete the pre-proceedings stage. Some have set up PLO panels that monitor the progress of the PLO cases, including those in the pre-proceedings stage.

Delay in pre-proceedings can be subject to scrutiny after the commencement of the care proceedings by the court. The children's guardian, who is appointed by the court as soon as the proceedings are issued, can critically analyse what occurred at the pre-proceedings stage and will bring to the court's attention:

- any delays that have occurred or possibly could have been avoided;

- what work has yet to be commenced or has not been completed in the pre-proceedings stage; or

- what further evidence is required, for example, independent expert evidence.

Consideration of the above is important for the court to know, in relation to case management decisions and directions that it may need to consider to progress the case now it has been issued and to ensure that there is no further avoidable delay. The court can be openly critical if delays could have been avoided, and if such delays will now impact on the care proceedings timetable.

A recent example of a local authority receiving heavy criticism and a costs penalty, due to a lack of progress of a case in the pre-proceeding stage, was clearly seen in the care proceedings commenced by Northamptonshire County Council.[8] Here, care proceedings were not commenced until some

---

8   *Northamptonshire County Council v AS and Others* [2015] EWHC 199

nine months after the child, DS, had first been taken into care at 15 days old. The judge was of the view that no satisfactory explanation was provided for the extraordinary delays. The judge explained the practical effect of the s.20 order in this case, which deprived DS of the benefit of having a children's guardian to represent and safeguard his interests. It also deprived the court of the ability to control the planning for DS and to prevent or reduce unnecessary and avoidable delay in securing a permanent placement for him at the earliest possible time. The judge made the unusual order requiring the local authority to pay £17,000 in damages for breaches under the Human Rights Act 1998. This case clearly demonstrates the importance of not allowing a case to drift, and that delay can be prevented by setting clear timescales and reviews so that the progress of the case can be carefully monitored.

The use of s.20 within the PLO process can be extremely beneficial in the care planning of cases in the pre-proceedings stage and, as identified earlier, it can have the ultimate effect that if a positive outcome is achieved, the child can be returned to the parents' or kinship care without the need to have issued care proceedings. However, the practice of s.20 should not be used as a way of controlling a placement and delaying without justification and with no real plan to issue proceedings. Such practice can be perceived as a misuse by the local authority of its statutory powers, as identified in the case of *Re N (Children: Adoption Jurisdiction)* [2015].[9] In *Re N*, the children were placed in voluntary care under s.20 in May 2013, but proceedings were not commenced until January 2014. Sir James Munby commented that s.20 may, in an appropriate case, have a proper role to play as a short-term measure pending the commencement of care proceedings, but the use of it as a prelude to care proceedings for a period as long as here was 'wholly unacceptable'.[10] Sir Munby also stated:

> The misuse and abuse of section 20 in this context is not just a matter of bad practice. It is wrong; it is a denial of the fundamental rights of both the parent and the child; it will no longer be tolerated; and it must

9   EWCA Civ 1112
10   Para 157

stop. Judges will and must be alert to the problem and pro-active in putting an end to it. From now on, local authorities which use section 20 as a prelude to care proceedings for lengthy periods or which fail to follow the good practice I have identified, can expect to be subjected to probing questioning by the court. If the answers are not satisfactory, the local authority can expect stringent criticism and possible exposure to a successful claim for damages.[11]

Under s.20, the parents retain parental responsibility for their child and the local authority does not acquire it unless it has been granted an interim or care order. However, once a child is accommodated under s.20, parents may feel that they have a limited say in their child's arrangements, including contact arrangements, education or even when the child can be returned to their care. It is therefore important for local authorities to work in a transparent way with parents, carers and family members during the pre-proceedings stage, and to apply the use of s.20, voluntary accommodation, in the correct way. This may assist with the parent's, carer's or family member's co-operation with the local authority and, if assessments are positive, could result in resolving matters without the need to commence care proceedings. Transparency from the outset can result in an increased level of trust between the local authority and parents, carers or family members, which could have the consequence of a better working relationship with fewer challenges once proceedings are issued.

Legal planning meeting

One of the key factors in achieving the 26 week timescale is for the local authority children's social care department to involve the local authority lawyers as early as possible. This can also assist in preventing delay and ensure early planning at the pre-proceedings stage.

The involvement of the local authority lawyers by the children's social care department commences with the convening of a legal planning meeting (LPM). As this may involve a cost to the department, the decision to convene

11   Para 171

a legal planning meeting may need authorisation by senior management within the children's social care department. The process may vary between local authorities, depending on internal charging policies and operational process. The social worker will need to consult with their own local authority's policies and procedures and ensure that the correct scheme of delegation is followed to authorise the convening of a LPM.

Once a local authority lawyer is allocated to the case, generally this lawyer will remain with the case until the conclusion of the proceedings. This will mean that a lawyer will support the children's social care department throughout the journey of the PLO process. It is therefore important for the children's social care department to keep the local authority lawyer informed of significant events so that the lawyer is updated and can properly advise on the legal course of action that should be undertaken. This will assist in the avoidance of drift and delay in the progress of the case.

A LPM can also be convened further to perhaps a recommendation of a child protection case conference, or by the children's social care department where the local authority has ongoing concerns about the care of the child. This course of action may be necessary after other plans and measures have been explored that may now not be deemed appropriate, perhaps because these have not resulted in positive changes or outcomes for the child. This may also be the case where the other measures were implemented and these have not been successful in keeping the child safe or well cared for and the children's social care department is now exploring the available legal options.

The purpose of the LPM is for the local authority lawyer to advise the children's social care department on the evidence and whether it meets the legal test of the threshold criteria, as set out in s.31 of the Children Act, which the court must be satisfied with before any family court can make a care or supervision order to a designated local authority in respect of a particular child. The legal test is:

- *That the child must be suffering, or is likely to suffer, significant harm.*

- *And that the harm or likelihood of harm must be attributable to one of the following:*

a) *The care given to the child, or likely to be given if the order were not made, not being what it would be reasonable to expect a parent to give; or*

b) *The child being beyond parental control.*[12]

The local authority lawyer will advise on any gaps in the evidence and whether further assessments should be considered, which could reduce the need to instruct independent experts. The lawyer may also advise on whether interagency documents are needed.

Many local authority children's social care departments now employ a case manager who will become involved in the case once the PLO process is commenced, just prior to or after the LPM. They will remain actively involved until the conclusion of the care proceedings. Their role is, in particular, to support the allocated social worker, to ensure that PLO timescales are met, and to provide quality assurance and consistency in the presentation of court documentation by the local authority.

Letter before court proceedings

If the children's social care department has been advised by the local authority lawyer that the threshold criteria have been met and senior management within the children's social care department have authorised the commencement of the PLO process, then the next step is to issue the letter before court proceedings. This letter is sent by the local authority children's social care department to the parents or carers with parental responsibility. The purpose of this letter is to act as a final notification to the parents or carers prior to the commencement of proceedings. It sets out the local authority's concerns, and the actions that are required by the parent or carer, failing which the local authority will commence legal proceedings.

The letter should include:

● the local authority's concerns and how these are evidenced;

12   Section 31, Children Act 1989

- what is required by the parents or carers to change and within what timescales;

- an invitation to the parents or carers to provide names of extended family members for the purposes of assessment as alternative carers;

- an invitation to the parents or carers to attend a pre-proceedings meeting.

The letter should be brought to the parent's or carer's attention and it is important that the recipients understand its contents. The letter should be written in plain English or, if English is not the parent or carer's first language, it should either be translated or sent at least with a paragraph in the parent or carer's first language, informing them that:

- they should not ignore this letter;

- they need to take action; and

- if they do not take action, the local authority can proceed with legal steps that can involve the local authority requesting the court for an order in respect of their child, which could result in the child being taken into care.

If the child's father is not actively involved in the child's life, the local authority should endeavour to identify the child's father and inform him of relevant information. If the social worker is unclear on what information to provide, advice should be sought from the local authority lawyer.

This letter is also important as it triggers the availability of legal aid public funding from the Legal Aid Agency (known as level 2 legal help). This is available to parents or carers who have parental responsibility; it is non-means tested and non-merit tested. As mentioned earlier, this means that if the parent or carer with parental responsibility instructs a legal aid-funded solicitor, they will be entitled to free advice and assistance. The recipient of this letter should be encouraged as a first step to seek independent legal advice from a solicitor who specialises in children law, and should be advised to consider instructing a solicitor accredited as a member of the Law Society Children Panel. Accredited Children Panel solicitors are recognised for their specialism in children law; their details can be found by contacting the Law

Society or visiting the Solicitors Regulation Authority website (see Useful Resources).

Pre-proceedings meeting

This is a meeting organised by the local authority children's social care department. It is an important meeting and is part of the pre-proceedings process. Parents or carers are invited to attend this meeting with their legal representatives. If the parents or carers have parental responsibility, they will be entitled to level 2 legal help; this legal representation will be funded by the Legal Aid Agency.

The purpose of this meeting is for the local authority children's social care department to discuss the contents of the letter before proceedings and to ensure that the parent or carer understands the local authority's concerns and what action is required.

The primary aim of the meeting is for the local authority children's social care department to reach a formal agreement with the parents or carers and to agree a plan as to how to bring about a change in the care of the child without the need to commence proceedings. This plan should include not only tasks to be undertaken by the parents or carers, but should also include actions that will be undertaken by the local authority, in particular in relation to what support will be available for the parents or carers. The progress of any action plan requires the full co-operation of the parents or carers. If co-operation is not forthcoming, then the risk is that the local authority can commence care proceedings with a possible care plan to remove the child if their safety, wellbeing or needs require this.

Family group conference

The local authority has a continuing duty to identify and consider placement with friends and family as possible alternative potential carers for the child if a child cannot remain in the interim or permanent care of their parents. This process of identifying possible carers needs to be undertaken as early as possible. One way to do this is by convening a family group conference.

Some local authorities will attempt to identify possible family and friends by convening either a family group conference or a family meeting as soon as the children's social care department becomes involved in the child's life. If it has not been undertaken earlier, the family group conference should certainly be convened in the pre-proceedings stage.

The concept of a family group conference was introduced as a formal requirement in the PLO in 2008 as a way of formalising the process of getting family members or friends to understand the concerns held by the children's department and to explore how the extended family or friends network could assist, and to see if any family members or friends would be willing to put themselves forward as possible short- or long-term carers.

One issue often raised by social care practitioners is that family and friends do not come forward early in the pre-proceedings stage. One of the reasons for this could be due to their belief that this may put them in competition with the parents and therefore it may interfere with the parents' chances to have the child returned to their care. This can result in prospective carers coming forward or parents nominating possible family and friends at a much later stage, for example, only when rehabilitation has been ruled out. This can then cause delay in the proceedings, taking them over the 26 weeks, and will also cause delay in the child being placed in a permanent placement.

One way to combat this problem is for the local authority, either with the allocated child's social worker or with the input of the family group conference facilitator, to assist parents, family and friends to understand that they are not in direct opposition to or even in competition with each other. It is important that those involved understand that the local authority needs to consider all realistic options alongside rehabilitation of the child to the parents' care within the child's timescales and, if proceedings have been issued, also within the court's timetable.

Once proceedings are issued, the courts may be requested to grant a direction that, if parents have not already done so, they should provide the local authority social worker with, say, up to two or three possible long-term carers whom they wish to nominate for assessment. If the parents fail to do this, then if carers come forward or are nominated at a later stage, the local authority could refuse to consider them. If the local authority refuses, then the parents can consider making a formal application[13] for an independent assessment of the prospective alternative carer. It will then be up to the court to evaluate and adjudicate upon whether the delay caused by undertaking the late assessment is justifiable.

In some areas, courts, in order to reduce the risk of family members being proposed at a later stage, are requiring the minutes of the FGC to be filed in the court proceedings so that it is clear what was discussed and what was proposed by the family.

Contact with a child in care

Duties to promote contact for a child in care are set out under s.34 of the Children Act 1989. Section 34(1) requires the local authority to allow reasonable contact with the child's parent. This duty remains until the child is made subject of a placement order.

Section 34(11) of the Children Act requires that:

> *Before making, varying or discharging an order under this section or a care order...the court shall –*
> > *Consider the arrangements which the local authority have made, or propose to make, for affording any person contact with a child to whom this section applies; and invite the parties to the proceedings to comment on these arrangements.*

If the parent who is party to the proceedings is not satisfied with the level of contact in care proceedings, the parent can apply for a contact order under s.34(3) of the Children Act 1989. The local authority will need to obtain an order under s.34(4) if it wishes to refuse the parent contact for more than seven days.

---

13   Application is made under Part 25 Family Proceedings Rules 2010

Review legal planning meetings in the pre-proceedings stage

The local authority children's social care department, as part of the review and monitoring process, may want to meet or keep in contact with other professionals involved with the child, the family or the parents or carers on a regular basis so that the agreed action plan is being monitored and progressed. As part of this review process, the children's social care department may also have regular legal meetings to ensure that legal action is not required during this pre-proceedings review process.

It should be noted that at no time does this pre-proceedings stage prevent the children's social care department commencing legal proceedings, should the welfare and safety of the child require this. Having regular reviews with the local authority lawyer will assist and support the children's social care department to focus on the pre-proceedings stage.

This review process is completely independent of any looked after children (LAC) review that the children's social care department is required to undertake for children who become looked after as a result of being brought into local authority care.

Commencement of proceedings

Care or supervision orders can only be commenced if the legal test is satisfied, as set out in s.31 of the Children Act 1989, the "threshold criteria".

If the local authority can demonstrate evidence on a balance of probabilities that the threshold criteria have been met, the court will then go on to consider the no order principle and whether making a care or supervision order would be in the child's best interests. Even if all the parties have reached an agreement in relation to the threshold criteria, the court still has a duty to satisfy itself that the threshold criteria for a care or supervision order have been fulfilled before making any order.

Prior to the decision to commence proceedings, the local authority lawyer will have already advised at the initial legal planning meeting whether the local authority has sufficient evidence to satisfy the threshold criteria. Once

KEY CHANGES TO FAMILY JUSTICE

the decision is made for the commencement of proceedings by the children's social care department, senior management and the local authority lawyer will advise on the court documentation that will be required to be prepared by the child's social worker.

The local authority will need to:

- complete the court application form C110A; and

- file annex documents.[14]

It should be noted that Form C110A now incorporates all applications for care, supervision and emergency protection order (EPO) applications. Therefore, it is possible for a local authority to lodge both for an EPO application, and also an application for a care or supervision order, on the same form and at the same time.

PLO Stage 1: issue and allocation

As discussed earlier, the court makes the decision as to which tier of judge will deal with the case once issued. Once the court has allocated the case, it will notify the local authority of the date, time, court venue and the judge allocated for the Case Management Hearing (CMH). If the local authority has a view, it can provide representations in relation to the allocation decision when the application form for care proceedings (Form C110A) is sent to the court. The other parties can also seek a review of the allocation decision after the court has made its initial decision.

In deciding on the tier of Family Court judge, the court will need to make the most effective and efficient use of judicial resources depending on the nature and type of application before the court. In terms of allocation, the court will consider the following factors:

- the need to avoid delay;

---

14 See below under the heading 'Court documentation' for more specific detail of the annex
    documents that are required.

- the need for judicial continuity;

- the child's or parties' location; and

- the complexity of the case.

Any tier of judge is generally authorised to hear care cases. Local authority social workers and managers will discuss the issue of allocation at the legal planning meeting and will be advised by the local authority lawyer as to which tier of judge would be most appropriate for their particular case.

It is important to note that no parties attend court at stage 1 of the PLO process.

Once the case is allocated to a judge, the allocation judge will then make standard directions, for example:

- compliance with the document checklist and directing any missing documents to be filed and served;

- appointing a children's guardian and ordering an initial CAFCASS case analysis by Day 10. If there is insufficient time, the children's guardian may give this orally;

- requiring the parents to respond to the threshold criteria document;

- listing the case management conference by Day 12 and a contested interim care order (ICO) hearing if required. The contested ICO hearing is listed either before the CMH or at the same time.

Contested interim care order hearing

If the local authority is seeking an interim care order and this is not agreed to by the parents, then the court will be requested to list a separate hearing by the local authority for a contested interim care order (ICO) hearing.

If urgent, this hearing can be requested by the court prior to the CMH. A contested ICO hearing may be urgently requested if, for example, the parent has withdrawn their voluntary agreement under s.20 of the Children Act 1989 and is insisting on the return of their child to their care. If the local authority is not in agreement then, in order to secure the child's continued placement, it will require an interim care order. The local authority will then seek an urgent contested ICO hearing so that the court can determine whether to grant an ICO.

It should be noted that if the child is in imminent danger, the local authority can commence emergency protection order proceedings in advance of any care proceedings, either at short notice or without notice to the parents, if the circumstances of the case require the child to be safeguarded immediately.

Interim care orders

One recommendation of the Family Justice Review was a simplification of the ICO renewal process. Previously, a judge or magistrates could grant the first ICO for up to a maximum of eight weeks; it would then be renewed for up to 28 days until the conclusion of the care proceedings. The renewal of the ICO had become an administrative process with the application being made by the local authority legal department and the court having been provided with rolling consents from the other parties; the court would renew the ICO for a further 28 days or to the next hearing date, whichever was earlier, unless consent was withdrawn. This has now changed.

Section 14(4) of the Children and Families Act 2014 amends the Children Act 1989 and removes the previous restrictions on the length of interim care and supervision orders as set out in s.38(4)(a) and (b) of the Children Act. This thereby leaves the decision regarding the duration of the ICO with the court and makes a more efficient use of resources. This change was made on the basis that the renewal of interim orders was rarely challenged and was often considered to be a mere formality due to the administrative nature of the process. Under the new changes, the court will be able to set the length of an ICO and or an interim supervision order (ISO) for a period that is considered appropriate. However, these orders cannot be made to last longer than the proceedings themselves and if they expire before the conclusion of the proceedings, the court can make a further order if necessary.

In practice, the court will make the duration of the ICO or ISO in line with the care proceedings timetable. This will then avoid the need for the court to make multiple interim orders within the life of the proceedings. These changes do not prevent any party from applying for discharge of the interim order by giving notice to the other parties, which will then require consideration for listing it for a contested ICO hearing.

PLO Stage 2: Case Management Hearing

The CMH takes place between days 12–18 from the date of the issue of the care proceedings. A full case management of the issues is to be undertaken at this hearing.

In order to be prepared for the CMH, parties need to use the time from the issue/allocation stage to prepare for the CMH. Parties can no longer come to court without a plan. To assist in the preparation of the planning of the case, the parties' lawyers will meet for an advocates' meeting to consider the issues that need to be either agreed or determined by the court. The parties' lawyers will attempt to agree a draft order or agreed directions that they can present to the judge at the CMH.

The CMH is a hugely important hearing and parties do attend court for this hearing. Social care professionals and, in particular, the allocated child's social worker should always attend with their diaries or details of their availability. This hearing will consider the filing of evidence to be timetabled together with the listing of further hearings, including the listing of the Issues Resolution Hearing (IRH).

The matters that will be considered at the CMH are as follows:

- the timetable of the proceedings to the IRH stage, if possible within the child's timetable;

- identifying the issues, including whether any of the issues can be resolved at this stage, particularly whether the threshold criteria or parts of it are agreed by the parent/s;

- if not already considered, then to consider whether a contested ICO hearing is necessary and if so, it is to be listed;
- consideration of kinship assessments;
- whether an independent expert is needed;
- whether any disclosure is necessary to other agencies, such as the police or the Immigration and Nationality Department;
- the local authority's plans and the available options.

In line with the spirit of the PLO, the judge will be proactive in ensuring that the parties have considered all that is necessary to progress the case without undue delay.

Further Case Management Hearing

A Further Case Management Hearing (FCMH) can be listed if necessary and if matters cannot be fully dealt with at the CMH. This should be the exception rather than the rule and should take place by Day 20 or Week 4.

A FCMH may be required where the parents have not yet instructed a solicitor. It may also be required due to the complicated nature of the case, for example, if it involves a non-accidental injury, and parties have not had an opportunity to consider the instruction of appropriate experts as further medical information may be outstanding in relation to the injuries.

Prior to the IRH

The local authority should endeavour to finalise its care plan by at least Week 16, in order to allow the other parties to respond to the local authority's final evidence prior to the IRH. If parties do file their evidence in time, this will result in having a highly effective IRH by Week 20.

The local authority has a duty to consider an early permanence placement. If the plan is adoption, the local authority needs to evidence that "nothing else will do" (see Chapter 6 on permanency planning). In order to present the final care plan, the local authority must have reached an analysis of all the available options so that it can finalise its final care plan by Week 16. This requires the social worker to undertake an analysis of all the realistic options. If adoption is the option presented to the court in the local authority's final care plan, then in order to progress this, the child's social worker will need to prepare the child's permanence report and present this to the local authority's agency decision-maker (ADM).

In order to achieve a decision from the ADM in time for the filing of the care plan, the ADM will consider whether adoption is in the child's best interests. If the ADM decides it is, then they must also advise that the local authority is to now make an application for a placement order. The local authority should then endeavour to have the placement order application issued prior to the IRH. If this application is issued, then at the IRH the court can direct that the placement order application should be consolidated with the care proceedings. If all the evidence is presented in relation to the placement order application in time, the care and placement order proceedings could be concluded at the same time, that is, within the 26 week timescale.

PLO Stage 3: Issues Resolution Hearing

The PLO introduced the Issues Resolution Hearing (IRH) as a new concept, in that this is now no longer a final directions hearing, but could, if possible, be utilised as a final hearing (that is, if it is possible to resolve all the issues at this hearing). The IRH will be timetabled at the CMH by Week 20. The purpose of the hearing is that if the issues can be resolved at this stage, then they will be, and if resolved there will be no need for a final hearing. For this reason, a final hearing is not set unless it is considered necessary at, or closer to, the date of the IRH.

As the IRH could possibly be used as a final hearing, it will usually be listed for a minimum of two hours up to a half day or a full day, depending on the time estimate provided by the parties' legal representatives. As is the case with the CMH, the parties' legal representatives are required to convene an advocates' meeting at least two days prior to the IRH. This will assist parties in considering whether issues can be resolved, and if so, which issues, to ascertain whether with limited evidence the matter can be finally determined at the IRH. If there is sufficient time allotted for the IRH, it is possible for the judge to hear evidence, including expert evidence or evidence from the parents or social worker on the specific issue/s that are in dispute. If the judge is required to hear evidence, he or she will have to be notified in advance of the IRH.

In order to attempt to resolve matters at the IRH, a clear analysis is required of those issues that the judge is being requested to resolve at the IRH stage and parties must come prepared for the judge to resolve them. However, if matters cannot be resolved at the IRH, a final hearing will be listed. In such a case, the court will give final case management directions at the IRH, such as:

- filing of threshold agreements or statement of facts or statement of issues remaining to be determined;
- filing of final evidence or amended care plans;
- filing of witness templates, agreed judicial reading list or reading time.

Final hearing

The final hearing (FH) must resolve all remaining issues and will be heard between Weeks 22–26, unless an extension has been applied for.

The judges and magistrates will be rigorous in processing cases so that the care cases can be completed within the 26 week timetable, unless they are considered to be exceptional.

The child's timetable

The 26 week timetable can be a challenge as there can be three timetables running alongside each other:

- the timetable for the child;
- the court's timetable; and

- the social work timetable, to comply with, say, internal local authority processes or procedures such as presentation to internal panels to secure funding, or authorisation for particular steps or resources.

These three timetables could run alongside each other, but may not be working together, which can be the real challenge.

The timetable for the proceedings, which is set by the court, is set having regard to the timetable for the child. The court will use the timetable for the child to assess the impact on the child's welfare. This takes into account dates that are important to the child's welfare and development.

Examples[15] of which dates may be relevant when setting this timetable for the child are:

- looked after children (LAC) reviews;

- dates relating to education stages for the child, for example, transfer to a new school;

- any health care steps, for example, assessment by a paediatrician or other medical specialist;

- any review of the local authority's care plan;

- any change in the child's placement;

- any significant change in the child's social or family circumstances.

The local authority is required to ensure that it identifies key dates relevant in the child's life in the application form C110A and for updates of this information to be included in the social work statements. Where the care proceedings relate to a sibling group, the court will set a timetable for each child, if it needs to differ. If the siblings do not have the same timetable, the court will consider the appropriate progress of the proceedings in relation to each child individually, for example, the start of a new school year will be an important date for all the children, but it will be even more significant

---

15 Paragraph 5.5 Practice Direction pilot practice direction 12A *Care, Supervision and other Part 4 Proceedings: Guide to Case Management*, 2013

for a child who is starting the GCSE curriculum. Equally, transferring from primary to secondary school will be a significant date when considering the placement plan for the child. So, for example, for a child transferring to a secondary school, the court may want to finalise the placement plan for that child, say, by July to allow sufficient time for applications to be made for the secondary school local to that placement prior to September and the start of the new school year.

How can the 26 week timetable be met?

The President has made it clear that the 26 week timetable is not a mean or an average, but the maximum time limit by which to conclude care proceedings. To achieve this, it is clear that the local authority has to endeavour to complete as much work as it can without delay in the pre-proceedings stage. Doing so will result in the local authority being in a position to "front load"; that is, to present the evidence, including assessments and possibly final care plans, at the commencement of the proceedings when the 26 weeks start.

To achieve the 26 week timetable, it will assist the local authority to attempt to do the following.

- The local authority should file and serve all required documentation at the issue/allocation hearing.

- The local authority should endeavour, prior to the commencement of proceedings, to have convened the family group conference, undertaken (or at the very least commenced) all necessary parenting assessments, kinship assessments or viability assessments.

- Once proceedings have commenced, the children's guardian is appointed and all parties should endeavour to have legal representation as early as possible. This will mean that if all parties are represented at the first advocates' meetings before the CMH, then all can have input in key issues prior to the CMH.

- If independent experts are being proposed, then parties should come prepared:
  - with the names of the proposed independent experts;
  - with the experts' availability and estimated cost;
  - to draft a letter of instructions or to draft possible questions for the expert.

- All of this information is needed by the time of the advocates' meeting prior to the CMH so that a draft order or proposals can be put before the judge or magistrates at the CMH.

Court documentation

When the local authority decides to issue an application for a care order or supervision order, the local authority needs to file the following documents with its Form C110A:

- a social work chronology for court purposes (some local authorities may file this as a separate document, some may include it in the social work statement);

- a social work statement, including a genogram (defined as a "family tree" that sets out in diagrammatic form the child's family and extended family members and their relationship to the child);

- current assessments relating to the child and/or family and friends of the child to which the social work statement refers and on which the local authority relies;

- a threshold criteria document (this is either filed as a separate document or is contained in Form C110A). The threshold document and the parent's response are limited to not more than two pages. This document is drafted by the local authority lawyer and approved by the children's social care department;

- an allocation proposal form and index of checklist documents (to be completed by the local authority lawyer).

Under the revised PLO, there is a requirement for focused and succinct court documentation, which means presenting only documents to the court that are relevant and significant. The President has advised that the court does not want any documents that are over two years old unless they are significant or if the local authority is relying upon them as part of their evidence. However, this does not mean that evidence is lost, as the local authority lawyers will prepare the documents under two categories: those that are to be filed with the court, and those that are to be listed (known as the checklist documents) and which exist on the local authority files.

The checklist documents are spilt into two categories:

- Checklist documents A – those that are to be served with the application, which will include evidential documents, such as:
  - previous court orders, judgements or justices findings, facts or reasons form;
  - any previous assessments or single, joint or interagency materials;
  - records of any key discussion with the family following, for example, a family group conference (FGC); some courts are directing that the actual minutes of the FGC be filed;
  - pre-existing care plans, such as "child in need" plans or protection plans;
  - letter before proceedings.
- Checklist documents B – those that are available to be disclosed on the other parties, if requested. If the other parties dispute any of the evidence in the listed documents, the parties can request this evidence to be included in the court bundle.

Social work legal chronology

The social work chronology contains a succinct summary of the significant dates and events in the child's life. It is found on the child's social work file and is intended to be a record of contact.

A separate chronology should be prepared for the court's purposes, and the President has advised that this social work legal chronology should consist of up to five pages, with the social work statement of similar length. This social work legal chronology is not the same as the social work chronology, as not all of the information on the social work chronology may be necessary to be included in the social work legal chronology that is for the court's purpose.

Whether it is a social work chronology or a social work legal chronology, they both need to be in chronological order with details of the oldest events leading to the most recent events.

Some courts locally may require the local authority to provide not just an initial social work legal chronology but also an updating chronology when filing subsequent documents. If an updating social work legal chronology is required, this should start from the date of the last chronology.

A chronology is an evidence-based document and should have sufficient detail so that it assists in presenting the evidence. A social work legal chronology does not require information listed in the same way as a social work chronology. Therefore, if the information is relevant it can be grouped together, rather than listing each item as individual entries. For example, in the case of listing every occasion on which the police were called to the family home (which may be how it is listed in the social work chronology), this information can be presented in the social work legal chronology by detailing, for instance, 'From date x to date y there were 10 call-outs for police assistance to the family home'.

It should be noted that documents filed with the court should not duplicate information; to avoid duplication, information can be cross-referenced. Therefore, the social work statement should not repeat information already contained elsewhere in the court documentation; this includes the chronology. The statement can cross-refer to other documents. Also, the social work analysis can include an analysis of the evidence that may be included in the chronology.

Witness statements

The PLO requires that where parties are relying on evidence or information that has been provided by a third person, it is preferred that the third person's evidence is filed in court as first-hand, direct evidence. This means that if, for example, there is evidence in a neglect case of direct observations from the child's school teacher, the health visitor or the home care assistant, then these professionals should be requested to provide statements detailing their observations to be filed in the court proceedings.

Social worker's statements

As discussed earlier, in care proceedings the local authority is the applicant and it must present evidence to the court to satisfy the legal test referred to as the "threshold criteria" pursuant to s.31(2) of the Children Act 1989. If the local authority satisfies the threshold criteria, this then entitles the State to intervene in a person's family life despite his or her right to respect for private family life (ECHR Article 8).

The court requires the social worker's statement to be less narrative, less descriptive of the history and to contain an analysis of the evidence. By using an analytical approach, it will assist the social worker in focusing on how the evidence impacts on the child. It also enables the social worker to demonstrate to the court and the other parties how the social worker has formed his or her professional judgement and recommendations. This analytic approach will assist in supporting the fact that the social worker is presenting evidence as a child care expert.

There is now a national Social Worker Evidence template that many local authorities are using or have adapted (see http://coppguidance.rip.org.uk/social-work-evidence-template/#SWET_templates- for further information). This template incorporates the *Re B-S* guidance and therefore its use or the use of any adaptation will ensure that the local authority's evidence will be presented and is *Re B-S* compliant (see Chapter 6 on permanency planning). There are helpful headings in the template to assist the social worker and guide them to the information that is needed. The social worker is required to provide this in a skilled, evidence-based analytic way. This analytical skill is critical for social workers to develop, not only in terms of presenting their evidence but also to demonstrate their expertise.

Care plans

Section 31A of the Children Act 1989 requires the local authority, in an application for care proceedings or a supervision order, to prepare a care plan for the child.

One of the recommendations of the Family Justice Review was that, although the court should play a central role in public law cases, the court did not need to scrutinise the care plan presented by the local authority as this can cause delay and duplication. The Family Justice Review suggested that the court should focus on the core issues of the care plan, as follows:

- whether the child is to live with their parents;

- placement with friends, family or alternative care arrangements; and

- contact between the child and family.

This recommendation was fully endorsed by the Government, which has resulted in in the introduction of s.15 of the Children and Families Act 2014, which amends s.31A of the Children Act 1989. This now requires the court to consider only the permanence provisions of the care plan, that is, where the child is to live.

The reason for this change is that Parliament took the view that local authorities (through the children's social care departments and the Independent Reviewing Officer (IRO)) were better placed to take forward the steps or resources set out in the child's care plan. If they were not carried out, there were sufficient measures through the IRO scrutiny process to monitor or review the care plan.

Therefore, the court is to specifically consider the "permanence provisions" of the s.31A plan, which is the local authority care plan in relation to with whom the child is to live:

- a parent; or
- any member or friend of the child's family; or,
- whether the child is to be adopted; or
- placed in other long-term care.

The court is not required to consider the remainder of the s.31A plan subject to the requirements under s.34(11) of the Children Act 1989, which still apples, thereby requiring the court to consider the contact provisions.

These limitations of course do not prevent the court from considering other aspects of the care plan, should it consider it to be in the best interests of the child to do so.

Court bundles

In care proceedings, preparation of the court bundle will be undertaken by the local authority lawyer. A bundle is required for each hearing. The changes in the PLO have also impacted on the reduction of the size of court bundles and new court rules set out the format that the bundle should take.[16] In particular, the court requires that, unless the court has specifically directed otherwise, the court bundle shall be contained in one A4-sized ring binder or lever-arch file limited to no more than 350 sides of text. If additional documentation is to be filed, the parties will have to seek permission before the relevant hearing and provide a good reason. These strict requirements need to be complied with, as set by the court, failing which, as the President has stated in the case of *Re L,*[17] the defaulting party will be named and shamed in judgements and could find themselves exposed to financial penalties.

The question may arise that with such court rules, is there not a risk that crucial evidence will be left out of the court proceedings? It should be clear that the

---

16   Paragraph 5.1 Practice Direction 27A, *Family Proceedings: Court Bundles (universal practice to be applied in the High Court and Family Court)*
17   *Re L* (procedures: bundles: translations) [2015] EWFC 15

rules do not prevent proceedings to be disposed of justly and so, if the evidence is significant and relevant, it should be contained in the bundle.

File on time

If any party has been directed by the court to file a document by a specific date, this must be adhered to. If the party is unable to do so, they must inform the court and seek the court's permission for further time, explaining the reason why more time is required.

Can experts be instructed?

The President has stated his view that social workers are experts:

> One of the problems is that in recent years too many social workers have come to feel undervalued, disempowered and de-skilled...If the revised PLO is properly implemented one of its outcomes will, I hope, be to re-position social workers as trusted professionals playing the central role in care proceedings which too often of late has been overshadowed by our unnecessary use of and reliance upon other experts.

The President's view is clear and his message has been passed to his lower judges. As judges accept that social workers are experts, they will not grant permission for the instruction of an independent instructed professional expert unless it is "necessary" to do so. If an independent expert is required, then s.13 of the Children and Families Act 2014 gives guidance on expert evidence and assessments in children proceedings. Section 13(1) of the Children and Families Act specifies that a person may not instruct a person to provide expert evidence for use in children proceedings without the permission of the court.

In general, the courts will be looking to children's social workers and/or the children's guardians to provide their "expert" opinion on social work-related issues, such as whether siblings should be placed together or separated, and placement options. Permission by the court will only be granted for the instruction of an expert if it is deemed to be "necessary" to resolve the proceedings justly. Section 13(7) of the Children and Families Act 2014 sets out the court's considerations when deciding whether to direct an expert's instruction. It is vital that parties' legal representatives ensure that all relevant information relating to the instruction of an expert is before the court prior to the judge making his or her determination.

Use of research evidence in the Family Justice System

Social workers can consider referring to research in their statements in support of their analysis. However, it is accepted that social workers can have legitimate fears in using research due to the difficulties in relating it to the specific circumstances of the case in question, and the fact that it could lead to protracted cross-examination on the subject. The social worker should consider taking advice from their manager and the local authority lawyer as to the advantages or risks of including research in their evidence and how those risks can possibly be reduced. If the social worker does include research, it is important to ensure that the research is relevant and significant and that it has not been superseded by more recent research. This may appear time consuming, but is necessary to assist with answering any questions in cross-examination by the other parties' legal representatives.

It is accepted that use of research evidence in family justice can be extremely helpful. The Family Justice Review made a number of recommendations in relation to sharing of relevant research and good practice.

The Family Justice Review in 2011 highlighted a need for:

- improved dissemination of up-to-date research and analysis on the needs, views and development of children;

- a system-wide approach to research and evaluation; and

- improved mechanisms for synthesising and vetting the quality of research in ways that are accessible and useful for practitioners, be they judges, legal representatives, social workers, CAFCASS officers, or members of local family justice boards.

The Government accepted these recommendations and the Family Justice Research and Analysis team in the Ministry of Justice Analytical Services are supporting this through the publication of the Family Justice Research Bulletin.

The research bulletin provides a summary of the findings of recent research relevant to family justice in England and Wales (private and public family law). It also has an international section. It includes information on current and forthcoming projects, providing useful links to fuller information (for example, Bulletin 5, published in January 2015, can be found at: https://www.gov.uk/government/uploads/system/uploads/attachment_data/file/398781/family-justice-research-bulletin-jan-2015.pdf).

In August 2015, the Nuffield Foundation announced that it intends to commission a scoping project to map the requirements for a solution which might improve the vetting, synthesis, dissemination, and translation into practice of research evidence and data relevant to family justice issues. It has started this process by hosting further discussions to inform the scoping exercise, to ensure that any solutions proposed successfully meet various stakeholder needs. These are all positive moves in assisting social care professionals to gain more confidence in using research evidence.

Advocates' meetings

As previously mentioned, advocates' meetings are usually held two days before the CMH and the IRH, to ensure that the legal representatives discuss and narrow the issues for the judge. It enables the legal representatives to present to the judge at the hearing either an agreed draft order or partially agreed draft order. If there is disagreement, then the areas of dispute between the parties can be narrowed for the judge to determine upon at the forthcoming hearing.

Only the advocates, that is, the legal representatives, attend this meeting, which can also be conducted over the telephone. Social workers and parents do not usually attend. The children's social care department and parents will be requested to provide an update to their respective legal representatives prior to the advocates' meeting.

Children's guardians

The role of the children's guardian is to provide an independent social work oversight on the case. They are expected to provide a case analysis at each significant stage of the proceedings, which will inform the court of the guardian's views at each stage, and to advise the court on what evidence or assessments may be required. This means that there will be less duplication of work between the local authority social worker and the guardians, as guardians are no longer undertaking social work assessments (this being the local authority social worker's role).

6

Permanency planning

The landscape of permanency planning has been impacted by two recent cases: *Re B (A Child)* [1] and *Re B-S (Children)*,[2] both of which have challenged social workers and children's guardians to examine their standards of analysis and how evidence should now be presented in the Family Courts. These cases and those that have followed do not change the law but have set in trend the current judicial approach to evaluation of cases where the care plan for the child is adoption with a clear focus on proportionality.

These cases further present a challenging reinterpretation of the interplay between the Children Act 1989, the Adoption and Children Act 2002 and the Human Rights Act 1998.

The approach now adopted in light of these two cases is not just restricted to those cases where the care plan is adoption, but all cases where rehabilitation to the parent's care is no longer being considered.

In *Re B (A Child)*, the Supreme Court stated that adoption is the "last resort" and only permissible if "nothing else will do". It also stressed that the child's welfare is paramount and that the child's interests include being brought up by their parents and wider family unless the overriding requirements of the child's welfare are such that this is not possible.

The President, in *Re B-S*, referred to a significant lack in the analysis of the options available for the child. The President stated that 'this sloppy practice must stop', and emphasised the need for a 'global, holistic and multi-faceted

1   [2013] UKSC 33
2   [2013] EWCA Civ 1146

evaluation of the child's welfare which takes into account all the negatives and the positives, all the pros and cons, of each option'.[3] Further guidance has been given that only the realistic options need to be considered, as opposed to all available options.

The court in *Re B-S* gave guidance that the evaluation of the options must not be a linear process, dismissing each of the options in turn until only adoption is left, but must be a real analysis of the pros and cons of each option. The President encouraged the use of a "balance sheet" approach, as suggested by Thorpe LJ in *Re A (Male Sterilisation)*.[4] This requires entries on each side of the balance sheet, listing the certain benefits and detriments of each option, followed by the potential gains and losses in each instance, making some estimate of the extent of the possibility that the gain or loss might accrue.

The impact of *Re B (A Child)* and *Re B-S*

- The starting point for all decisions about a child must be that of the child's welfare being the paramount consideration. *Re B (A Child)* reminds us that the child's interests include ideally being brought up by their parents or wider family, unless the overriding requirements of the child's welfare make that not possible.

The Supreme Court in *Re B (A Child)* makes it clear that severance of the family ties inherent in an adoption without parental consent is an extremely draconian step, that adoption must be considered as a last resort, and that it can be appropriate only when "nothing else will do and when all else fails". To satisfy this last criterion, the social worker's analysis must show that the needs of the child for permanence and stability within an adoptive family outweigh all of the positive elements identified as being available through ongoing connection with the child's parents or wider birth family.

- Before the court makes a decision that will separate a child permanently from their birth family, the court must be satisfied that all the realistic

3   Para 40
4   [2000] 1 FLR 549

options, including the provision of necessary support or services, have been fully considered that would enable the child's return home, or to be cared for within his or her own extended family. This requires consideration of:

- whether there are any services that would provide the requisite assistance and support;

- that the child has the adequate protection for him or her to remain within the care of the family; and

- whether the family is likely to engage with those services.

Social workers, in their evidence, should consider and, if appropriate or relevant, identify any services or support needed to enable reunification. So, if relevant, consideration should be given as to whether those services can be provided, how they will be provided and whether they will be accepted and used by the child's parents. The court will be alert to any possibility that resource implications might play a part in the placement decision. The President, in *Re B-S*, directed judges to be particularly rigorous in questioning the local authority's thinking if they suspect that resource issues are influencing the care planning for a child. Equally, there is no merit in providing services that do not properly address the family's difficulties. The willingness and ability of parents to accept ongoing intervention and to use any services provided to effect and sustain a positive change for the child must be included as part of the analysis of the possibility of return home.

In considering the possibilities of a successful return home, protective factors need to be set against risk factors in the "balance sheet".

In the case of *Re B (A Child)*, the child was not returned home to the parents' care because the court accepted the local authority's case that the parents' personalities and history were such that they would be unable to co-operate with any protective services.

- In *Re B-S*, the court was clear in that it did not require local authorities to undertake further assessments, nor was it expecting a duplication of information. What the court requires is that the available information is properly analysed and the conclusions justified. The analysis must be evidence-based and focused on the facts of the case. It should include analysis of all the possible options, and provide clear conclusions and recommendations adequately reasoned and supported by evidence. If sufficient evidence is not available before the court, then further assessments or independent expert reports could be requested or directed, which may lengthen proceedings so that the court can fully consider the expert reports or further assessments prior to making its decision. This could impact on the court's timescales and cause delay in the final determination of the case.

On a practical note, the social worker is not expected to list in their statements all available options but only the relevant or realistic options for the child. Therefore, in practice, it may be that only two or three options are possible realistic placement options for a child, and it is only those that need to be considered. However, it is extremely important for the courts, for the parents, and ultimately for the child, that it is clearly understood in the social worker's statement as to why one placement option has been given preference over the others. The statement must include an analysis of each realistic option having been carefully considered, with the positives and negatives balanced in a way that puts the child's welfare at the centre of the decision-making process.

- The issue of proportionality in the context of adoption is important. The case of *Re B (A Child)* highlighted the interplay between the Children Act 1989 and the Human Rights Act 1998. A judge cannot properly decide that an order should be made unless the order is proportionate, bearing in mind the requirements of ECHR Article 8, respect for family life and the interference in the child's life. Therefore, an adoption order will only be proportionate if "nothing else will do".

- *Re B-S* made it clear that the fact that the child has been placed with prospective adopters or lapse of time cannot be determinative factors, nor can the mere passage of time. The case also stressed that judges must not attach undue weight to the adverse impact on the prospective adopters and thus on the child. However, the court will consider the age and characteristics of the child, and the longer the child has been placed with the prospective adopters the greater and the more adverse the impact of disturbing the arrangements is likely to be.

- The judge must always bear in mind that what is paramount in every adoption case is the welfare of the child "throughout his life". Given present life expectancy rates, this means that, with a young child, one is looking far ahead into a very distant future, upwards of 80 or even 90 years. Equally, judges will be careful not to attach undue weight to the short-term consequences for the child if permission to oppose the adoption order is granted.

- The Court of Appeal acknowledged in *Re B-S* that in the short term there would be substantially more appeals in relation to adoption cases and that probably more of them would be successful. Across the country, local authorities are experiencing an increase of parents attempting to apply for revocation of placement orders, leave applications and opposing of adoption proceedings in light of this recent case law and the judicial approach currently being given in such applications. It should be noted that for the parents to be granted leave to bring an application, they have to simply evidence a change of circumstances either in their lives or the child's life, which then compels the court to consider whether or not they have any prospects of success. Those changes of circumstances do not have to be significant or substantial. The consequence of these applications has resulted in reopening of cases or lengthy contested adoption proceedings.

- Placement orders were introduced in the Adoption and Children Act 2002. They were designed to consider dispensation of parental consent prior to the adoption proceedings and to provide an element of certainty and a sense of assurance to local authorities and for prospective adopters when children were placed with them. The effect of these two cases and subsequent cases is that this confidence has been impacted upon, resulting in being considered as a possible barrier for prospective adopters to initially come forward. If prospective adopters do proceed with their adoption application, there is a possible further risk that they could find themselves as respondents in direct opposition with the child's parents.

- As a result of this level of uncertainty, information given to the child needs to be considered very carefully, particularly the points below.
  - A child's understanding when placed with prospective adopters may be that this placement is their "forever family". Life story work may have been undertaken whilst in foster care to prepare the child for their "forever placement". Social workers will need to consider what information to provide to the child at the point of placement and whether information should be limited, reserved or qualified until the adoption order is granted.
  - It should be carefully considered whether children should be told that the final direct contact with birth family members at the time of placement with the prospective adopters is the final goodbye/farewell contact.
  - Changes in language or approach in the information provided to the child and/or the prospective adopters may result in a degree of uncertainty until the adoption order is granted. Such uncertainty will impact on the ability to recruit more adopters, which does not support the Government's agenda to speed up the adoption process.

- There is an increased risk of potential for delay before an adoption order can be made if the court grants the parent's application for leave even where placement orders have been made and even when the child has been placed with prospective adopters. This again goes against the Government's current expectations in respect of adoption.

- Local authority social workers carry a greater evidential burden with a requirement for the presentation of a clear analysis and exploration of all available realistic options, including the availability of local authority support. Without this, it will make the plan for adoption more difficult to achieve and open up the possibility of the parent's ability to have the case reopened at a later stage.

- There has been an increase in other permanency options, such as special guardianship orders and even placement with parents whilst the child remains subject to care orders.

How can local authorities minimise the impact?

Local authorities may be reassured that the risks can be minimised initially by submitting analytical evidence that is *Re B-S*-compliant and robust care plans in the care and placement order proceedings.

1. It is accepted that local authorities do not consider care plans for adoption orders lightly and will only propose such a plan if all other options, including placement with kinship carers, have been fully explored. The Supreme Court's decision in *Re B (A Child)* supports the same approach and strongly suggested that local authorities must explore all possible alternatives before final orders are made. Before making the final order, the court must be satisfied that there is no practical way of the local authorities or others providing the requisite assistance and support to the parents or family members to provide the parental care required. Robust evidence and clear analysis of this exploration will be required to be provided by the local authority in the care and placement order proceedings.

2. Delay in finalising the child's permanency plan could be further mitigated with firm judicial case management of any applications by birth parents, and with clear directions sought by the local authority, including in relation to the filing of expert and other assessments.

3. The President indicated in *Re B-S* that the guidance in this case is to be followed as good practice. He stated:

    We have real concerns, shared by other judges, about the recurrent inadequacy of the analysis and the reasoning put forward in support of the case for adoption, both in the material put before the courts by local authorities and guardians but also in too many judgements. This is nothing new. But it is time to call a halt.

To assist social workers and the courts, a new national template has been introduced (as previously mentioned) and local authorities have been invited to use it. This will assist in presenting evidence in future cases and ensuring that they are *Re B-S*-compliant, which will mean less opportunity for possible applications by parents for the reopening of cases, and that these applications will be less successful or will not get past the leave stage.

It is recognised that the recent case law has had an impact on the reduction of numbers of adoptions and increase in special guardianship orders and kinship care placements. At the time of writing (January 2016), the Government has announced that it is now considering legislative change to adoption and strengthening special guardianship assessments. Until the exact changes proposed are known, it is too early to consider the impact of these changes, and whether they will have the impact of speeding up the process for adoption, as is this Government's priority.

7

Adoption and early permanence planning

Early permanence planning is a term used to describe both Fostering for Adoption (also known as Fostering to Adopt) placements and concurrent planning.

Fostering for Adoption

Fostering for Adoption is used where the local authority is of the view that rehabilitation to the child's parents is no longer a viable option and adoption is the only plan. However, in order to progress this plan, it requires permission to place the child in a prospective adoptive placement. Such consent can be provided by the child's parents themselves or the court can give this to the authority with the granting of a placement order. Until such consent or authority is acquired, the local authority cannot place the child within an adoptive placement.

However, a child can be placed with carers who are dual-approved both as foster carers and prospective adopters. With this dual approval, the child can initially be placed with the carers as a foster placement. Once the local authority has permission to place the child in an adoptive placement, the local authority can take steps to change the status of the carers from foster carers to prospective adopters, thereby reflecting the child and the carers' correct legal status.

Fostering for Adoption placements suit particular types of cases and carers; therefore careful consideration must be given as to whether a Fostering for

Adoption placement is to be pursued. Once the decision has been made to place the child in a Fostering for Adoption placement, the focus will be on the child and the carers, and not on the parents. There will be no further consideration by the local authority to undertake any further assessments of the parents. It is therefore important for parents to ensure that they identify all potential friends or family carers at the earliest opportunity so that all possible placements are considered before the local authority pursues a Fostering for Adoption placement.

The clear benefit of this type of placement is that the child remains with the same carers without any disruption in placement, even when the legal status of the placement changes. This is of course important as the child will not have to create new attachments and can build on those that they have formed with their carers, which in turn will help the child to form strong attachments in the future.

Very helpful practice guidance has been produced by Coram and BAAF (2013). Further information can be found at: www.coram.org.uk/how-we-influence-practice-and-policy/our-fostering-adoption-guidance.

Concurrent planning

Fostering for Adoption should be distinguished from concurrent planning. With Fostering for Adoption, there is no further work being proposed by the local authority to be undertaken with the child's parents. Once the decision has been made by the local authority that adoption is in the child's best interests, the child will be moved to the Fostering for Adoption carers.

Concurrent planning is different in that whilst assessments are still being undertaken, it allows the child to be placed with foster carers who may become the child's long-term carers after the local authority has explored all other permanency options, including rehabilitation to the parents' care. Concurrent planning requires foster carers who are willing to work with the child's parents towards rehabilitation, and only if this is ruled out will they then be considered as prospective adopters for the child.

The benefit of Fostering for Adoption placements is that the other options, including rehabilitation, are ruled out and the child's care plan is adoption with limited possibility of disruption of the child's placement. With concurrent planning there is more uncertainty, as other options are still being considered.

With either Fostering for Adoption or concurrent planning, the local authority will have to inform the court and the parties of the nature of the child's placement. If any other party, including the child's parents, is not in agreement, the opposing party has the ability to challenge this placement plan, by requesting the matter be set down as a contested hearing, which means that the court will have to make a decision. It is important for the local authority to be able to evidence that prior to consideration of the Fostering for Adoption or a concurrent placement, all other realistic options, including assessment of viable friends and family placements, have been considered. It is important for the local authority to obtain the court's approval of the care plan, including the placement plan, as although the court does not have the power to order the local authority to make a specific fostering placement, it does have the power to decide whether to grant the local authority an interim care order and can refuse to grant this. Without an interim care order, the local authority will not have the authority to decide on the placement.

Section 2 of the Children and Families Act 2014 amends s.22C of the Children Act 1989[1] by making it a duty for local authorities to consider Fostering for Adoption or concurrent planning in certain circumstances.

Statutory guidance requires that:

- parents who are providing voluntary agreement under s.20 of the Children Act 1989 must be fully informed of the local authority's consideration of placement in either a Fostering for Adoption or concurrent placement;

- the local authority also has a duty to ensure that the parents also fully understand the consequences of giving consent to such a placement;

- if the parents do not agree, they can refuse to consent, thus requiring the local authority to issue proceedings so that the local authority can obtain

1   Section 2 of the Children and Families Act 2014 came into force on 22 July 2014.

the court's permission for the placement. Form C110A includes a section that requests information on whether the local authority is considering adoption, to include details of the application for a placement order and, if it is not accompanying the application, information on when it will be submitted.

Ethnicity

Section 1(5) of the Adoption and Children Act 2002 required the adoption agency to give due consideration to the child's religious persuasion, ethnic origin and cultural and linguistic background.

There were concerns that social workers felt constrained by the statutory provision as specified in s.1(5) and were waiting unnecessarily to find prospective adoptive families that shared the same ethnic background as the child.

The Department for Education was concerned about the delay that this could cause for children and so provided draft Statutory Guidance on Adoption (2013c) which states that:

> Any practice that has the effect of stopping a child from being adopted primarily because the child and prospective adopter do not share the same racial and cultural backgrounds is not child-centred and is unacceptable.

This was then reinforced in statute with the repeal of s.1(5) by s.3 of the Children and Families Act 2014 (with the exception of Wales).

Local authorities should inform parents about the prospective adoptive placement and provide information to them as to how the identified prospective adopters will promote the child's ethnic, religious, cultural and linguistic background. If the parents are not satisfied, they can voice their objections to the local authority. The local authority may not be restricted by such objections if it is able to demonstrate that the child's ethnic needs have been considered and that steps will be taken by the prospective carers in promoting the child's needs in the short and long term.

Adoption and contact

Section 9 of the Children and Families Act 2014 inserts a new s.51A and s.51B in the Adoption and Children Act 2002. Prior to these amendments, if a person was seeking contact with an adopted child, they would firstly seek permission from the court to make an application for a contact order under s.8 of the Children Act 1989. As discussed earlier, contact and residence orders under s.8 have been replaced by child arrangements orders; separate changes were therefore made for those orders relating to adopted children.

Under s.51 of the Adoption and Children Act 2002, the court has the ability to make a contact or a no contact order when either making an adoption order or after an adoption order has been made. These new provisions can also assist adoptive parents who wish to prevent or stop informal contact, say, for example, via social media. The Act lists categories of persons who can be named in such orders, as follows:

- a person who, prior to the adoption, was related to the child by blood or half-blood, marriage or civil partnership;

- a former guardian of the child;

- any person who had parental responsibility immediately before the adoption order was made;

- any person with whom the child lived for one year, which does not need to be continuous but does need to be within five years before the application is made.

With the new provision came a certain level of uncertainty from adoptive parents that with the increase in categories of persons who can be named in such orders, this would lead to an increase in applications for contact orders. However, this has not been the case. There are restrictions on the availability of legal aid as these are private law proceedings. Further, it should be noted that in order to proceed with the application, the applicant must first seek permission from the court (unless the applicant is the child) and the court will consider:

- the applicant's connection with the child, adopter or prospective adopter; and

- any risk the proposed application may have in disrupting the child's life.

Adoption support services

Section 5 of the Children and Families Act 2014 inserts a new s.4A into the Adoption and Children Act 2002. After a local authority has carried out an assessment under s.4 of the Adoption and Children Act 2002 for adoption support services and has decided to provide any adoption support services to the adopted person or the adoptive parents, the local authority must prepare a personal budget for the person.

Section 6 of the Children and Families Act 2014 inserts a new s.4B into the Adoption and Children Act 2002 (which came into force on 25 July 2014). This requires local authorities to provide specified information about adoption support services. This is to ensure that information is available from the outset to those persons who may be interested in adoption.

8

Fostering: Staying Put arrangements

If the child has remained in foster care, and meets the criteria under the Children (Leaving Care) Act 2000 and on reaching 18, he or she will become a former relevant child; the child is entitled to the benefits of Staying Put. This allows the young person, once he or she turns 18, to remain in their foster placement if this is also agreed by the foster carer. This concept is not new to local authorities, as they were already required to develop a Staying Put policy.[1] The change is that this is now incorporated in statute by s.98(2) of the Children and Families Act 2014, which inserts a new s.23CZA into the Children Act 1989.

As Staying Put arrangements are now incorporated in statute, this has clearly strengthened the concept and ensured that there is now consistency between local authorities nationally. To assist social care professionals, the Government has produced guidance: The Children Act, Guidance and Regulations, Volume 3: *Planning Transition to Adulthood for Care Leavers* (DfE, 2010, revised in May 2014) and *Staying Put: Good practice guide* (The Children's Partnership, 2014).

---

1   The Children Act 1989 Guidance and Regulations, Volume 3: *Planning Transition to Adulthood for Care Leavers*

9

Carers, disabled children and young vulnerable adults

In addition to the recent changes introduced with the Children and Families Act, changes that relate to children and families have been dovetailed within those introduced in the Care Act 2014.

The Care Act 2014

The Care Act is another far-reaching piece of legislation and is one of the most important pieces of adult social care legislation; it has been long awaited and replaces much of the previous legislation, including the National Assistance Act 1948 and the NHS and Community Care Act 1990. The Act provides a single legal framework in the area of adult social care needs for adults and support for carers. This Act requires local authorities to adopt a whole-family approach, co-ordinating services and support around the person and their family and considering the impact of the care needs of an adult on their family, including children within the family.

Children who are carers

Census statistics in 2011 revealed that there are 166,363 young carers in England, compared to around 139,000 in 2001. One in 12 young carers is caring for more than 15 hours per week. Around one in 20 young carers misses school because of their caring responsibilities (ADASS *et al*, 2015).

In recognition of the increasing number of young carers, ss.96 and 97 of the Children and Families Act 2014 insert new sections at s.17ZA to s.17ZC of the Children Act 1989, which require the local authority to undertake an assessment of young carers.

A young carer is defined in s.17ZA(3) of the Children Act 1989 as a person under 18, who provides or intends to provide care for another person and if it appears to the local authority in England that:

- a young person may have a need for support; or

- it receives a request from that young person or parent of them, to assess the need for support.

The local authority will need to carry out a Young Carers' Needs Assessment to consider what support the young carer may need, even if the assessment is not requested.

Young carers in transition to adulthood

Sections 63–64 of the Care Act 2014 require a local authority to undertake a needs assessment of a young carer if it considers that:

- he or she is likely to have needs for support after reaching the age of 18; and

- that the assessment would be of significant benefit to him or her.

If the local authority decides not to undertake such an assessment, it must give reasons for its refusal.

Care of disabled children

Section 97 of the Children and Families Act 2014 inserts new sections at ss.17ZD to 17ZF of the Children Act 1989 that relate to the assessment of those carers with parental responsibility who have care of disabled children. The duty to carry out an assessment of these adults is triggered where it appears to the local authority that the carer may have support needs or that a request is made to the local authority from the carer for an assessment.

The assessment will be undertaken if the local authority is satisfied that the disabled child and his or her family are persons to whom "children in need" services can be provided under s.17 of the Children Act 1989.

Parent carers of a disabled child in transition to adulthood

Sections 61–62 of the Care Act 2014 place obligations on local authorities to assess the disabled child's parents during the transition of the disabled child to adulthood. The Act requires a local authority to undertake a needs assessment of the carer of a disabled child if it considers that the carer is likely to have needs for support after the disabled child becomes 18 and that the assessment would be of significant benefit to the carer. Such an assessment is referred to as a "child's carer's assessment". If a local authority decides not to undertake such an assessment, it must give reasons for its refusal.

Continuity of support for disabled children/young carers in transition

Section 67 of the Care Act 2014 requires that the assessments of disabled children/young carers take place before the young people become 18, and will continue to apply when disabled children/young carers become 18 until the assessment is reviewed. If the local authority does not treat the assessments as a continuing obligation, then the local authority must reassess.

10

Education

Virtual heads

Another concept that will not be new to local authorities is the virtual head. The key change is that this is also now incorporated in statute. Section 99 of the Children and Families Act 2014 inserts new subsections 22(3B) and 22(3C) to the Children Act 1989, requiring local authorities to appoint an officer as a virtual school head. The role of the virtual school head is to monitor and track the educational progress of looked after children. The virtual head can also be requested to assist and liaise between the social care professionals and the school for the child's benefit. It should be noted that the virtual head does not have any contact with the child directly and only liaises with the professionals.

Education Health Care Plan

The Children and Families Act 2014 creates a new "birth-to-25 years" Education, Health and Care Plan (EHC) for children and young people with special educational needs. This replaces the special education needs process, and the new process offers families personal budgets so that they have more control over the type of support required. When a person turns 18, in some cases the "care" part of the EHC plan will be provided for by adult care and support, under the Care Act 2014.

Conclusion

These family justice reforms have been termed by the President as:

The largest reform of the family justice system any of us have seen or will see in our professional lifetimes.

The former Justice Minister Simon Hughes stated that:

For too long children have suffered from excessive delays and confrontational court battles. Our reforms will keep families away from negative effects of battles or delays in court and make sure that when cases do go to court they happen in the least damaging way.

The changes implemented by various legislation detailed in this guide are far-reaching, focused on children's needs at the heart of these reforms. The reforms mark a significant moment for the family justice system. These are interesting times. The process of change has begun; however, it should be noted that it has not ended but is an ongoing process for the benefit of children and families.

Appendix 1: LA pre-proceedings practice: good practice essentials

Early work with the family	Concerns escalate	Legal gateway/planning	Final decision	Application and evidence
EARLY WORK WITH THE FAMILY Consistent, focused work with family, including multiple agency inputs where appropriate, to ensure children's needs are met and that they can be brought up within their family wherever possible FGCs/family meetings to identify wider support available and potential carers Planned interventions and support offered reflect evidence-informed practice and clear view of the child's needs Progress and impacts on the child rigorously monitored, assessed and recorded Improvements required and by when made clear and consistently communicated	**CONCERNS ESCALATE** Potential to move to proceedings subject to managerial review Early, direct and frank communication with parents on potential for proceedings Action required to avoid this made clear and, where appropriate, additional support provided Early planning set in train in case proceedings prove unavoidable Key sources of evidence including views of the child collated and updated; additional family carer assessments commissioned Outline case summary prepared; decision-making meetings provisionally scheduled in	**LEGAL GATEWAY/PLANNING** Evidence reviewed – are threshold and other tests met? Alternatives to proceedings appropriately explored? Assessments up to date or are other assessments needed? (If appropriate) Further attempts to support family/retain the child at home	**FINAL DECISION** Where concerns are confirmed, processes and timing for completing essential pre-proceedings work with the family agreed Does parent have capacity to instruct a legal representative? Parent/s told of concerns in a way they can understand and invited/ encouraged to respond. This to complement the formal letter and meeting before proceedings (If appropriate) Specialist assessment discussed and agreed with parent/legal representative	**APPLICATION AND EVIDENCE** Social work statement contains clear evidence to support the core judgements which the court has to make Evidence is balanced/reflects the degree of certainty with which conclusions have been reached Documentation screened and quality assured by senior social worker All essential annexed documentation submitted by PLO deadlines All questions in the application form adequately addressed

Reproduced from work undertaken by ADCS (see http://adcs.org.uk/care/article/public-law-outline-2014-update)

79

Appendix 2:
Public Law Outline 2014 (26 weeks)

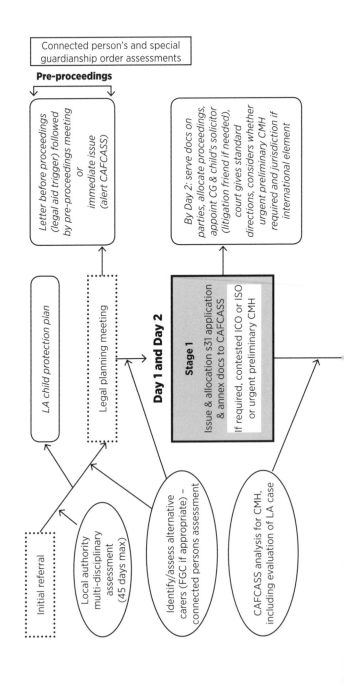

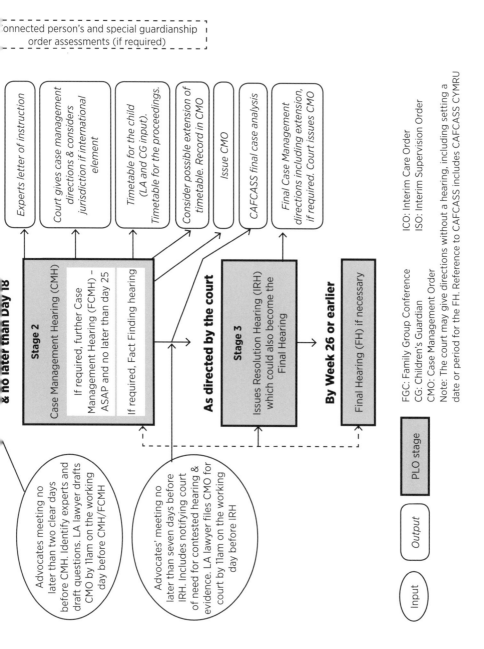

Connected person's and special guardianship order assessments (if required)

& no later than Day 18

Stage 2
Case Management Hearing (CMH)

If required, further Case Management Hearing (FCMH) – ASAP and no later than day 25

If required, Fact Finding hearing

Advocates meeting no later than two clear days before CMH. Identify experts and draft questions. LA lawyer drafts CMO by 11am on the working day before CMH/FCMH

As directed by the court

Stage 3
Issues Resolution Hearing (IRH) which could also become the Final Hearing

Advocates' meeting no later than seven days before IRH. Includes notifying court of need for contested hearing & evidence. LA lawyer files CMO for court by 11am on the working day before IRH

By Week 26 or earlier

Final Hearing (FH) if necessary

Experts letter of instruction

Court gives case management directions & considers jurisdiction if international element

Timetable for the child (LA and CG input). Timetable for the proceedings.

Consider possible extension of timetable. Record in CMO

Issue CMO

CAFCASS final case analysis

Final Case Management directions including extension, if required. Court issues CMO

FGC: Family Group Conference
CG: Children's Guardian
CMO: Case Management Order

ICO: Interim Care Order
ISO: Interim Supervision Order

Note: The court may give directions without a hearing, including setting a date or period for the FH. Reference to CAFCASS includes CAFCASS CYMRU

Input

Output

PLO stage

81

References

ADASS, Department of Health, Local Government Association, The Children's Society and Carers Trust (2015) *The Care Act and Whole-Family Approaches*, London: ADASS *et al*

The Children's Partnership (2014) *Staying Put: Good practice guide*, London: The Children's Partnership

Coram and BAAF (2013) *Fostering for Adoption: Practice guidance*, available at: www.baaf.org.uk/webfm_send/3217

Department for Education (2010) The Children Act, Guidance and Regulations, Volume 3: *Planning Transition to Adulthood for Care Leavers*, London: DfE

Department for Education (2012a) *An Action Plan for Adoption: Tackling delay*, London: DfE

Department for Education (2012b) *Support and Aspiration: A new approach to special educational needs and disability: Progress and next steps*, London: DfE

Department for Education (2012c) *The Government Response to the Modern Workplaces Consultation*, London: DfE

Department for Education (2013a) *Further Action on Adoption: Finding more loving homes*, London: DfE

Department for Education (2013b) *More Great Childcare: Raising quality and giving parents more choice*, London: DfE

Department for Education (2013c) *Draft Statutory Guidance on Adoption: For local authorities, voluntary adoption agencies and adoption support agencies*, London: DfE

Family Justice Review Panel (2011) *Family Justice Review: Final report*, London: Ministry of Justice, DfE and Welsh Government

Lord Chancellor's Department (2002) *Scoping Study on Delay in Children Act Cases: Findings and action taken*, London: Lord Chancellor's Department

Ministry of Justice (2014) *Action Research to Explore the Implementation and Early Impacts of the Revised Public Law Outline (PLO)*, London: Ministry of Justice

Ministry of Justice (2015) *Family Justice Research Bulletin* number 5, London: MoJ, available at: https://www.gov.uk/government/uploads/system/uploads/attachment_data/file/398781/family-justice-research-bulletin-jan-2015.pdf).

Ministry of Justice and Department for Education (2012) *The Government Response to the Family Justice Review: A system with children and families at its heart*, London: MoJ and DfE

Munby J (2013) 'View from the President's Chambers: the process of reform', *Family Law*, 548

Munby J (2014a) *Transparency in the Family Courts: Publication of judgements practice guidance*, available at: www.jordanpublishing.co.uk/system/redactor_assets/documents/1171/transparency-in-the-family-courts.pdf and www.jordanpublishing.co.uk/system/redactor_assets/documents/1173/transparency-in-the-cop.pdf

Munby J (2014b) *Transparency – The Next Steps: A consultation paper issued by the President of the Family Division*, available at: www.judiciary.gov.uk/publications/consultation-family-transparency-the-next-steps/

Useful resources

Care Proceedings Programme, Ministry of Justice (2010) *Your Child could be taken into Care: Here's what you need to know*, available at: http://webarchive.nationalarchives.gov.uk/20130128112038/http://www.justice.gov.uk/downloads/protecting-the-vulnerable/care-proceeding-reform/parents-pack.pdf

A booklet for parents whose children could be taken into care, which provides information about the legal process and what parents have to do at each stage.

Solicitors

Details of specialist solicitors can be found by contacting the Law Society on 020 7242 1222 or at www.lawsociety.org.uk, or using the find a solicitor fuction at: http://solicitors.lawsociety.org.uk/. The Solicitors Regulation Authority website also provides details of solicitors who specialise in children law: visit www.sra.org.uk.

Family Rights Group

An organisation that provides a free telephone and email advice to family members who are involved with children's services about the care and protection of their children.

Advice line: 0808 801 0366
www.frg.org.uk/

Coram Children's Legal Centre

Provides free independent legal advice to children, parents, carers and professionals.

Advice line: 0300 330 5480
www.childrenslegalcentre.com
http://childlawadvice.org.uk/

Glossary

ADM	Agency Decision-Maker
CAFCASS	Children and Family Court Advisory Support Service
CAO	Child Arrangements Order
Children's guardian	also referred to as a guardian. The guardian is appointed from CAFCASS. The guardian will be appointed once care proceedings have been commenced.
CMH	Case Management Hearing
EHC	Education, Health and Care Plan
EPO	Emergency Protection Order
FCMH	Further Case Management Hearing
FDAC	Family Drug and Alcohol Court
FH	Final Hearing
ICO	Interim Care Order
IRH	Issues Resolution Hearing
IRO	Independent Reviewing Officer
ISO	Interim Supervision Order

Litigants in person	A person who is a party and is representing themselves without the assistance of a legal representative.
LAC	Looked after child/ren
LPM	Legal Planning Meeting (convened by the local authority)
MIAM	Mediation Information and Assessment Meeting
McKenzie Friend	Someone who assists a litigant in person with their case. The McKenzie Friend does not have to be a lawyer or have any legal background.
PLO	Public Law Outline